Scared of Something Different

Journey of Business Disruption and Innovation

By Keith Churchouse and Esther Dadswell

© June 2016

1

SIGN HERE,
HERE AND HERE!...

JOURNEY OF A FINANCIAL ADVISER

Keith Churchouse

THE RECESSION
IS OVER

TIME TO GROW

Keith Churchouse

NAGGED,
TAGGED AND BAGGED

THE JOURNEY OF RECOVERY

Keith Churchouse

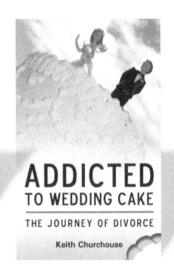

ADDICTED
TO WEDDING CAKE

THE JOURNEY OF DIVORCE

Keith Churchouse

#MAKEITHAPPEN

The Fifth Churchouse Chronicle ©

First Edition

ISBN 978-0992828127

Further contact details and information can be found at www.churchouseconsultants.com

**No financial advice of any description is offered
or deemed to have been provided
during the text of this book.**

**No legal advice of any description is offered or deemed to
have been provided during the text of this book.**

Some of the names, titles, sequencing, areas and dates in this book have been amended to ensure that this work portrays a personal experience rather than those of individuals or companies. Any similarity is purely coincidental. This book is also an expression of the personal opinion of the author.

For reference, SaidSo.co.uk is a trading name of Chapters Financial Limited, which is authorised and regulated by the Financial Conduct Authority, number 402899.

A donation will be made to the charity Headway Surrey for each book sold.
Registered Charity No: 2991672 / www.headwaysurrey.org

I hope you enjoy!

Acknowledgements

Vicky Fulcher

Our biggest thanks go to Vicky Fulcher who has embraced with vigour our world of work and all its diverse nuances. You have furthered our cause and for this we are humbly grateful.

Karin Walker

Esther and I have worked with Karin Walker for over a decade and our world is a better place for it. Her straight talking and direct approach are always refreshing in a world that needs focus to ensure that it delivers. Her innovations to her business are a testament to her forward thinking and I am delighted that she was able to share some of her learning along the way.

www.kgwfamilylaw.co.uk

The Chapters Financial Team

The champions of all we achieve.
As individuals, they are powerhouses of learning and wisdom.
With a shared cause, they are powerful and allow thoughts and ideas to grow and reach new plateaux that are far easier to reach together than individually. My sincere thanks to them.

www.chaptersfinancial.com

Translation Team

To Suzana Chazan, our love and respect for being part of our writing team in allowing us to diversify the text to far greater markets, such as the wonderful country that is Brazil. Our warm thanks to Valeria and to Suzana for sharing our journey of literary discovery.

Friends and Colleagues

To our contacts, colleagues and friends, we thank you for sharing your wisdom, knowledge and understanding with us.

Graham Booth and Fiona Cowan

You have both been with us from the very start, adding great value to the text and designs we achieve for our books. You put up with our many amendments and tolerate and share our fastidious attention to detail. Thank you for all you do for us as a publisher and as a business.

www.creationbooth.com

wordsbird.wordpress.com

The wonderful team at Kyan

Our innovation process would not have existed for the development of SaidSo.co.uk without the dynamic web development team at Kyan. Thank you for your patience and professionalism.

www.kyan.com

Reproduction Consents

Thank you to those organisations that have allowed us to reproduce documents and diagrams, details of which may be found in the Resources section at the end of this book.

Resources & Referencing

*As with any good innovation, many references are made to sources from the internet, rather than from other books. We have added these in **Resources** under the heading Resources & Referencing. We are not responsible for the content of the internet text. However, it may provide extra insight into your journey of disruption and innovation.*

Contents

Scared of something different

Foreword by Esther Dadswell

BEng (Hons),CEng, MICE, CMgr, MCMI

So, what now?

How do you feel about what you have achieved with your business enterprise or SME? Have you had time even to stop and think about it? Are you proud, engaged, tired, frustrated, even excited? Now that it's up and running, established, viable, even profitable, what are you planning next? I hope you have some new plans.

When focusing on real innovative change, as we have, this book often refers to our experience in UK retail financial services. However, we believe that our journey is relevant to *all* business models, across a huge spectrum of industries and services.

The easy option would be to carry on doing the same as you've been doing until now. Sadly, these dynamic times don't afford such a luxury to any business that still wants to be profitable in a decade's time. I am not alluding to getting someone to refresh your tired website and giving them permission to wander on to Twitter for you. I'm suggesting a real upheaval of all or part of your business, to turn it on its head, to shake every part of it to see how it could be working differently, more profitably, quicker, cheaper. What is going to be your new key selling point?

The help for start-ups always has been significant in the UK, for pro-digital businesses and tech hubs, and for all the other trendy businesses that come and go; that 'underdog' entrepreneurial spirit that favours the upstart business with a 'can-do' spirit coming to the fore. But what about the majority of SMEs, the ones that put in the hours, week in week out, the backbone of UK plc, that are largely ignored by the business media while they move through their growth cycle? Maybe once they have clocked up a decade or so of grind, they believe they know what they are doing by now... or just never stopped to look around and see where they are... or where they might be going. Let's face it, that original business plan might well have run out five or more years ago, and the ego trip of the owner has long since subsided... If you could start all over again, would you want to start from where you are now?

The change from established to innovative is harder for those who have been around for a few years, ingrained in their standard business model, and probably not the focus of government initiatives to get them 'off the ground'. You are *already* off the ground; you just need to reach for the stratosphere. That's why it requires new thinking, new challenges, and greater deviation from the current norm. What are you going to do about it, and what are your competitors going to do to fight for your hard-won market share in this new, innovative and disruptive market? It's up to you; it always was. However, it's not as hard as it first appears, if you plan and apply yourself.

Early adoption of technology and the way you apply it to your business will be key to its future success. The internet and what it can achieve for you is still in its infancy and the Fourth Industrial Revolution has only just dawned. Time to wake up and make a day of it! Your newly inspired successes won't happen overnight, and although there might be some immediate development cost, the benefits will be clear in your accounts in two-three-four years' time and thereafter. Influence what you can. Influence and don't waste time with matters that you cannot change. It is a waste of your energy otherwise. But you must also accept that there are no limits to what is now possible.

Now it's your turn. This moment of opportunity, to break through the ceiling of your business's current income stream, to challenge your modus operandi.

I know what I'm talking about. I have been there, done that and got the T-shirt. I have personal experience of the toil it takes to make it happen in an aspirational SME. Two major points of solace are that you are not alone in this quest and that, importantly, no one has found The Answer… yet! But you have to take the journey to find out, and be ready for change, however it may appear or be indicated to you by the end user. For it is the end user that will give you the winning answer — and it may not be what you expected.

Reflection

In reflecting on the journey in co-writing this book, I have used many inspiring words. This is in itself a reflection of what is a very inspiring subject. It is each of our individual and very personal takes on creation, innovation and disruption that shape the final outcome of our quest to make things better. Each one of us has a passion for certain subjects and the way we approach them. Sharing this wisdom with others allows different shapes to occur, which can prove to be even more inspiring than the original plan. Often the outcome far surpasses the original plan. It's sometimes fun to reflect on when the original plan disengages from the new, to form what you now have as your next evolution, leading to the position that there is no limit to what can be achieved. And that's a great place to be.

You will find a section in the book, confirming one vital innovation and disruption position. It says: 'Because you can!' and you should always have this at the forefront of your mind, ethos, ethic and outlook. The energy you will need to breathe life into your new thinking, to persuade others along the creation phase that it will work and still find the energy to deliver and market your business 'baby' is paramount. Personally, I refer to this as 'the colour of business innovation and disruption'. Fresh, pure, clear, dynamic, exciting and more. Never lose sight of this — and if you think you might, then print it out and put it next to the place that you work best.

The Fourth Industrial Revolution

You are not alone in your quest. This was re-confirmed in January 2016 by the World Economic Forum in Davos. As they state: *We stand on the brink of a technological revolution that will fundamentally alter the way we live, work, and relate to one another. In its scale, scope, and complexity, the transformation will be unlike anything humankind has experienced before.*

They refer to this as the Fourth Industrial Revolution.

The Third Industrial Revolution, around 1969, used information technology and technology to automate production. The Fourth builds on this still further, being cited as the digital revolution and the fusion of technologies, blurring the lines of digital, physical and other spheres. Awesome!

Know that your timing could not be better in looking at your part of the world, wherever that is on the globe. Having capacity for global reach for your creation is inspiring indeed. This all brings challenges, but also creates fresh opportunity on top of the opportunity you'd already spotted.

So, what now? More of the same? No problems if that's what you'd planned... but here's the key: *did* you plan it? At least stop to think about it before the next decade disappears with little direction and it's already too late. You've done the hard work, you are well established and you have golden years ahead of you... if you get it right.

Be assured that the world will innovate and disrupt around you anyway. It's just a question of how much you want to be a part of it and build forward.

Scared of something different

Preface

You already knew you were good! You didn't need to start a business to prove it, but you were ready to do that at the time. Now, if you have time to reflect, it's clear that it was the right decision. Yes, it was a bit of an egotistical whirlwind at the outset, and why wouldn't it be?

The business has grown, matured and perhaps even become a bit comfortable by now. Inspirational innovation and business disruption are there to be explored and embraced. There aren't many challenges that you have not seen before, there's cash in the bank, profits are reasonable, cash flow is fine (with the odd 'pinch point', where everything troublesome seems to happen simultaneously at the wrong moment), the bank still likes you, and your family still know who you are. What's not to smile about?

So, you ask yourself, what's next? The World Economic Forum suggested in January 2016 that this is the Fourth Industrial Revolution. Wow! What an era to embrace. What a time to lead your business through new opportunities, through the next few ticklish years to a higher, even more dynamic level. Disruption, innovation and revolution as business phenomena are still in their infancy and your company needs you to introduce them now more than ever, irrespective of which industry or profession you favour.

You do have the option to stand still, of course, although I hope this would seem unnatural to you, as both a business and a business leader. You now need to shake it up, to do something that pushes your boundaries, creates positive disruption, to drive you on.

Or… are you scared of something different? Just like during those awkward teenage years (both personal and business), what worked before doesn't cut it any more. Frustration, even anger, sets in, signalling that it's time to redefine who you really are and to start innovating as you move forward. The gap in the market that your business once filled as the new upstart all those years ago — and that made you so successful — has closed up and been reinvented elsewhere. Did you move with it? Did you follow your market, or did you break the mould, innovate and become the market leader yourself?

It is time that you refocused, re-engaged and redefined what your business can really achieve with the new technology, methods and distribution channels that are readily and affordably available to you now. Just like at the start of your enterprise, no one except you is going to push that business through the next few transitional years. You can't stand still because that would mean unwinding all your good work. The same-old, same-old ritual is not going to work anymore. Technology and its distribution opportunities have transformed business in the last decade... and they haven't even scratched the surface! Read this book and take a giant leap forward. Don't let yourself down, don't be disrupted, be the *disruptor*. Innovation doesn't stand still, and nor should you. You've worked too hard to let it all slip now.

Preface

Scared of something different

Chapter One: Expectation

Expectation: *a strong belief that something will happen or be the case*

Expectation of the future birth of our creative, and at the same time disruptive, plan was so exciting. Naivety played a part in my view of the opportunity, to transform the delivery of our business model through the use of new technology. I found it inspiring at the start and this has never waned. It is not difficult to understand that our main business, UK retail financial services, is not normally found in the top ten of anyone's life 'bucket list', but it is nonetheless a necessary process. Indeed, many similar professions can, in my opinion, be enlightened by creativity and innovation; it only needs a willing character full of expectation to take the leap into the unknown.

The thrill of this expectation has only been equalled by the reality of the additional two-year journey we have taken over the prior project work that had been achieved in the decade before. The reality of our project has proved infinitely better and bigger than I could have ever dreamt. To me, however, this is a significant point. Had I and the team not gelled together, to take those initial steps, we might not have achieved what we set out to do, let alone gone the extra miles that we have since travelled.

The personal development has been inspiring and now, when I have expectations again, they are far greater than they ever used to be — partly because I have learned what can *really* be achieved. I hope to share some of this learning with you in the pages to come.

As you know, the team and I are involved in UK retail financial services. However, this journey of disruption and change is relevant to *all* businesses and industries, irrespective of their type or size.

The personal challenges abound and they are exactly that: *challenging*. You become more robust as you overcome each of them, and so does your new offering and the way that it moulds itself to the planned solution. The 'eureka' moments are fabulous and the sleepless nights and 'pinch points' less so, but these are all part of the expectation of creativity, of innovation, of disruption, and of course of *success*.

Detractors will do their thing, adding a measure of derision along with their 'wisdom'. Others will observe what you're doing with admiration and their own expectations of what you are really achieving and delivering. Mark both of these responses well; you will need them both while you incubate and grow your new inspired solution.

Enough of the same!

To look forward, to innovate, to disrupt what has gone before, you have to look back (hopefully not for long) and consider junctions in your business journey where, had the processes and technology that are now available to you been available back then, you might have taken a different course. That is not to say that you went wrong.

You did what you could at the time *with the assets you had available to you* at that point.

Are you hard-wired into the same old thinking? You can change a few things, address a few problems, gain a quick win every now and then, control the odd setback? Do you still believe that change is only needed when it's needed... and that it's not needed very often?

Let's think about now. Often the results that some people achieve from their businesses stay the same. The easiest way to consider and map this position is to look at the annual accounts. You may well see a trend of the same income, same gross profit, and the same yield to the directors/owners. Holding your business ship steady is a good thing, even admirable. During the recession, some would argue that it was the *only* thing to do. If there are significant variances in the accounts, why? You may want to set a tolerance of say 5% per annum, to see what falls outside of these margins, and a thorough quizzing of the past accounts is always worthwhile. That alone may point to profitable years, and those which were less so. You may be able to spot opportunities. This checking will become increasingly important if you need to finance any changes, because any lender, old bank style, or new challengers such as peer-to-peer lenders, will certainly go through the same process before making any offers.

For example, our net profits in the past year have fallen because of the significant investment we made into financial technology, culminating in the launch of our new dynamic online proposition. The reduction makes sense and is in line with expectations from our planning.

In previous years we saw one significant stage step-up in income. Why? Because we made changes to our fee model that took around a year to work their way through, but which then filtered into the accounts, increasing profits. Great, but it was all down to planned and managed changes that affected the core of the company. 'Enough of the same!' I hear you shout; and I would agree.

It might seem counter-intuitive to turn any well made plans on their heads, but it is always worth looking at a plan from a different angle before deciding how you are going to implement the final version.

Challenging what went before in your business is vital to making production different in the future. Again, this is not to say that the past business plan or management was incorrect. I have a saying: *'If I could start again, I would not choose to start from here!'* Think about this for a minute or two. If you were to innovate, would you start from where you are now, or could you start from another base that would be a better place from which to launch? There is nothing stopping you from starting wherever you want to. Perhaps you could look at two scenarios, starting from where you are and where you dream you could be. When we started our main company, I set out to create a small business, great at what it does, bespoke and exclusive. And now, I have exactly what I asked for and discover, with hindsight (that exact science!) that to some extent, it is *not* what I wanted. I would prefer to have had a larger company. Admittedly, I am a lousy people-manager, so it is probably just as well that I have what I do have. But if I could have my time over again, with the new technology available to me, I would… well, I'm sure you get my meaning.

There should always be 'eureka' moments in business, when you suddenly think: 'We should try this.' It would be a pretty dull place if they never happened! You are an entrepreneur after all; the person that others rely on to come up with brilliant ideas, and more importantly, to implement them. The standard 'completer/finisher' position is the one where many people falter. If you're not the person to see it through to the end — and sometimes this is not the most exciting part of any innovation — you should package the idea as far as you can take it and hand it over to a member of your team who *will* see it through.

You must be able to trust them to be fastidious in their approach, to make sure they do not detract from the innovation. The simpler the innovation, and its approach or process, the better. Attention to detail in delivery is everything, so check and check again before launching. And, if your endeavours in the past did not manage to get it off the ground, ask yourself *why not?* Could they succeed now, do you think, with a different approach or application?

Many companies make changes to leadership. Previous ideas that never came to pass before are reborn and are a great success. If you *are* that old leader, look behind you at what could have been done differently... and dare to implement it now.

When you slide into your workplace tomorrow, or even tonight, and it envelops you like a comfy jacket — familiar, warm, possibly threadbare in places (but there's nothing wrong with that, is there?) — you need to understand that you might be in the wrong place. In my opinion, few people can truly innovate from a place of comfort and familiarity. This is precisely the mould that we are trying to break.

Pick up the phone and make a call to someone under the age of twenty. They will wonder what on earth you are doing calling them. Don't you know how to text, email… anything other than actually talk in real time? The world is moving on, techniques are moving on, disruption is occurring and you need to embrace it.

Take that jacket off now, before you get too cosy!

Stay on course

However you work, don't change any agreed or planned business course because of emotion. Emotions are powerful, personal and never to be underestimated. I know this from direct experience: emotion can affect important decisions and plans. Those emotions accurately reflect the prevailing mood of you, your business or your industry — or all three — at the time. The feelings might be of hope, fear or greed, or a combination of others. Whatever they may be, they will be personal to you and at the core of your thinking.

Emotions need to be managed, to ensure that they are controlled when delivering a planned strategy. They also create additional uncertainty, which is the mainstay of innovation and disruption. Uncertainty is going to be your partner anyway. You don't need emotion confusing your project processes further. Remember, the only party you want to be emotive and to be thrown off-course, dazzled in the headlights of the new offering, is the end user. There is purpose to your work. Stay on course and save all that emotion for the post-delivery/launch event.

Energy breeds energy

Did you ever meet one of those really annoying 'life is fab' and 'yes we can' types who extol the virtues of positivity, even when the muck is hitting the fan? They are welcome when you want to climb out of a dip in your own energy levels, but why must they be like that *all the time*? How do they do it?

There is an old saying, however, that '*if you want a job done, give it to a busy person*', and there is truth in this. Identify these traits and use them. The trick is to be able to separate positive from negative energy, and to apply each in proportion to maintain positive outcomes. This creativity, even excitement, of developing a new enterprise based on the old model, has created extra energy in our main business.

Energy can be positive or negative, even dark, and it all needs careful channelling. I refer to *dark energy*, because it is very hard to find, hidden in corners of your mind, and can be the most powerful if you can extract it from there and bring it into the light. It is a part of you, the inner core of the belief that your innovation will work. It might take a virtual 'cerebral collider' to express it to the world — but if that's what it takes to make it happen, so be it.

Treasure this energy, any cerebral energy and capacity that is available to you. In particular, treasure the cerebral energy that is more powerful than physical energy, but less obvious. We use our brain every waking second and the time we use it and what we focus on is vital to being successful. Do not clutter your time with triviality when you should be concentrating on the core principles of the disruption you want to cause... or even avert... with clever planning.

Even if you do get entrenched in your thinking and can't easily self-motivate your way out, go and find that über-positive person I mentioned earlier. Buy them lunch or a drink and then feed off their energy. It is contagious I can assure you!

Know that you are changing, that it's going to happen, that it's all about where you place yourself

Whatever approach you take to the evolution, innovation and hopefully revolution of the model you plan to launch, or develop further, there will be detractors. Genuinely new ideas often create fear in others. This is to be anticipated and I refer to these people as 'energy zappers'.

Imagine you have a meeting or give a presentation offering new inspiration or 'value-adds' to a project. The words that excite you so much start to flutter round the room like bright butterflies, teasing your colleagues, delighting some of them and, of course, being swatted by others, the detractors. There was no advantage to them in stopping the inspired idea, other than to stop progress, initiative and possibly value. However, the view of the detractors *does* add value in guiding you towards what will and will not make a difference.

The naysayers will always be delighted to give you the benefit of their so-called wisdom, whether requested or otherwise; rarely do they compete to *inspire*. Their energy is used to stop things, rather than to let them forge ahead. Engage with these people if you must, but never let them slow your project and goals. Eventually it is the end users who decide, who will judge your product by the purchases they make, or by the business that you sell.

Some people might argue that there are too many books on innovation and disruption — possibly the very idea-swatters we've just been talking about. Innovation and disruption are such vast subjects that I am not sure there could ever be enough, as long as they represent the truth of what's happening here and now. Even these inspired and exhilarating times will pass, with books for the memories, and the outcomes of experiments in disruptive innovations which have since become the norm. But it is just that: experiment, disrupt, deliver. Innovation and creativity will not happen without it... or without you.

It's our time to change the world!

Treasured print readers

Let me give you an example of change. I recently emerged from a session on my computer screens to grab a sandwich, mentioning to my colleague along the way that by early afternoon the newspapers do not seem to sell well these days. I'd noticed how many broadsheets and tabloids seemed to stay untouched in their display stands. I'd had my fill of news from various sources at my desk, and on returning to my chair I thought no more about it. That afternoon, the announcement reached me that the newspaper, *The Independent*, was to move to an online-only model, abandoning altogether the printed version. In a letter to readers the editor observed that the close of print would occur in around a month's time from the announcement, and that for their 'treasured' print readers, the new option *'doesn't appeal too much'*. The major part of the announcement for me was: *'The simple fact is, there just aren't enough people who are prepared to pay for printed news.'*

There has for some time been speculation that many of the current printed newspapers will not survive in their present physical format, evolving initially to digital-only space, before finally progressing to a digital subscription-only business model. Some people are surprised that it has taken this long to see the first major industry casualty. Indeed, I have personally questioned the economic viability of printing this book, rather than restricting production to e-reader options only, almost as the default. The newspaper announcement also had, in my opinion, the sense of a business having waited too long to embrace change, when demand and profits were clearly shrinking around it.

Change is hard, there is no doubt about that. However, even if a customer or end user is 'treasured', the world is shifting and business models have to move with the times or consign themselves to the history books.

A new printed newspaper opened to great fanfare, shortly after the closure of *The Independent*, and then promptly closed about two months later.

Hissy fits are part of the fun

Throwing a hissy fit, as you might call it when a child throws a tantrum, is never becoming in an adult. Some may suggest it demonstrates a deep-seated immaturity that is not suitable in a business owner or manager. However — and this is only my opinion — when you are innovating and creating, you are likely to be digging into your very soul in order to disrupt previous thinking, to challenge it, and effectively to throw it out. It's exhausting, but exhilarating at the same time! Other people are likely to challenge such thinking and planning; this may lead to some discord during this process of creation.

We certainly found this to be the case over the months of development when we went through the process in my own business. Seeming almost juvenile at times, frustrations ran strong and continually needed to be countered or out-thought in order to come up with new thinking and solutions. Swearing, at times, was not uncommon. I was relieved to see in a recent press article that this is a recognised behaviour in the intelligent. Indeed, an article in the *Language Sciences Journal*, produced by psychologists Kristin Jay and Timothy Jay in late 2015, indicates that a fluent use of profanity can be a sign of an articulate nature and a deep intelligence.

I'm never one to argue with science!

So, in your development process, if a hissy fit happens, go with it. This doesn't mean it will always work. However, it can demonstrate urgency, even impact, and if the team has a common purpose to succeed, these 'pinch-points' are to be expected. It may also be the start of the next great segment in your innovation.

Never as complex as a human

New technology invariably brings streamlining, or automation. Computers and machines are complex, but not as complex as humans. Some see this in itself as a challenge.

Innovation should advance, rather than reduce, our progress. It is soul destroying to find your work being outdated, overshadowed and then finally crushed by new methodology and thinking; only to find that the new ways, although they are undoubtedly forward thinking, do not work as well as the old. But by then, as you know, it's too late for you. Someone innovates, possibly by the use of modelling or automation, only to hit the underlying reality that humans are the best computers in the world, and that they cannot be replaced in full. China, I understand, is finding that automation is making millions redundant, but they too will evolve.

Global Business Review produced an article in April 2015, entitled: *Robotics Making Workers Redundant in China*, about real examples of automation in large factories, to improve quality, but at the same time making many employee roles obsolete.

Does it make you cringe?

While I was preparing notes for our new project website, one of my colleagues cringed at the liberal wording I was planning to use for some user guides. I carried on, knowing that I was on the right lines. To be honest, our office and its team are a bit, well, educated and *posh*. Even I sometimes wonder how I managed to get mixed up in such cerebral company. There is nothing wrong with that, as long as you know that you're probably not going to reach in communication terms the 'average person on the Underground'. If the average person is not your target market, then this is not a problem, but it's a different thing if they *are* your broader target. One person's view can be the acid test, alerting you to something that might repel another person.

That colleague's horrified response to my view on a particular issue was, in principle, reassurance that I was on the right lines. Have you ever met someone and, no matter what they suggest, you instinctively head in entirely the opposite direction? Recognising your own position can be a powerful tool in thinking about the demographics you are trying to engage with, the demographic that you already work with, and as in the case above, the gap between the two.

You may also need to think about how far your innovation could go. Is it designed for a target market locally, or for a niche market in a locality, possibly a city? And who is limiting this target: you or the product or the end user? Could it be used nationally or internationally? All the better if it can, but does this opportunity create a diversification in the demographic that you need to appeal to? The world is your oyster, but if you can't reach the end user, you definitely do need to adjust your message.

We make these subconscious choices every day. Where we work, what we wear, how we speak, where we shop, our potential changeability, who we socialise with... these are the choices we each make all day long. All choices, the preferences that fundamentally define us, probably define the group we associate with, add an element of a demographic. All these potential aspects need to be observed and considered if you are to engage with the end user you are targeting with your innovation, especially if it is a new disruptive model... and I hope it is.

So, the next time a colleague cringes at an idea, respect their views. When you know that colleague 'X' turning his or her nose up at a suggestion is the acid test, go with it! Alternatively, if the new concept doesn't make you, or them, feel awkward, ask yourself: *has it gone far enough*? You may want to consider this challenge further and apply solutions accordingly.

Scared of something different

Chapter Two: Passion

Passion: *strong and barely controllable emotion*

Could a definition be any more correct, than when it comes to the lust to make a business concept fly? You will know that business is about passion, not just doing a job! Successful, engaged business innovation is about living and breathing life into every aspect, every corner, of the new commerce you support. It's a bit like eggs and bacon: one is involved, the other is *committed*! Which one are you?

A new idea, concept, design needs renewed passion from start to finish and beyond to make it thrive. This is because if you are going to disrupt current thinking, current applications, you are going to be challenged and denied regularly and your energy and belief is going to be the difference between its success, or its consignment to the memories of but a few. This is a long process and passion will need to be with you throughout.

There is nothing stopping you. You just need imagination, creativity, energy and passion, mixed together with a large amount of tenacity, common sense, reality and business acumen. It might be fair to suggest that this is quite a lot to ask, but if you don't do it now, at the dawn of the

Fourth Industrial Revolution, someone else who is less capable than you will, and you cannot stand by and let that happen.

Accept the challenge with passion.

...Because you can!

In writing a book, I diversify my life in terms of time, but also in terms of my thinking. This communication is both cathartic and rewarding, whilst also being challenging. So, why do I do it? I have detailed some of the merits, but one important point is simply... because I can!

In 2009, along with our main business, we established a publishing company — hence this book, in case you hadn't guessed. We are the controlling partners within the business. If I want to write and publish a book, I can. What have you done within *your* business which also allows *you* access to diversify what you do into other avenues? The 'because you can' principle. Although rather forced down this route by a publishing industry that was in disarray at the time because of many economic pressures, led by the recession and technology in the form of e-readers disrupting the paper book market, there was a theme, certainly for us, of *'scared of something different?'* The answer was *no*, but we still had to hold our nerve.

If you think about the varying aspects of your own business, I would apply screens to each segment that you identify:

- What are you good at, and not so good at? Hopefully you know this and the reality is that you are brilliant at everything! ...but are you? Challenge yourself. You might want to create a scoring system to do this.

- What products, services or processes are the most profitable and the least profitable? Again, score the process. You will understand that we are looking here at the 80/20 rule of profitability.

- Finally, what area puts a spring in your step every morning, and what area, if you could afford to lose it tomorrow, would you willingly scrap? It's only because of 'XYZ' reason, possibly profitability, that you don't.

Challenging yourself, without beating yourself up or being obsessive, is good. However, now ask your fellow directors, partners, senior managers to do the same and see what results you get. If you dare, ask your most trusted clients to do the same. Their views and inputs are vital, although you may want to put it in the context of improving business services first to ensure you don't spook them.

Now, compare your notes against the other results to see what synergy you get, or not as the case may be. This alone may show you where to target your planning, with the potential to digitise a service, aiding performance and profit.

For example, our traditional mainstay business focus is on people over the age of fifty. Why? Because they have invariably accumulated wealth and are 'coming in to land' for retirement. It is particularly at this *de-cumulation* stage where our business adds real value. As a consequence of this, we do not offer much service, or significant value, to those in the *accumulation* phases of life, invariably twenty-five to fifty years old. Yes, we set up savings plans, recommend funds and contribution levels, adding in great value where we can, although there are some limits.

Potentially it's a bit short sighted of us (and possibly underestimating what we do). However, resources are stretched at one lucrative end of the business, to cater for the demands of the work flow, to offer a great proposition at the other end. Or at least, that's what we thought until we disrupted the model and looked at low cost, easily accessed alternatives. This is where our online proposition now adds new focus.

No one has The Answer

It has started to become clear that, although the revolution in the online financial advice market we are part-leading is evolving quickly, no one yet has The Answer. Each emerging solution has a variation on a theme in its proposition and this is to be expected, even encouraged. Business would be a bit dull if someone just came up with an answer and we all rolled over and accepted that solution. Indeed, the real power of the internet is that the end consumer decides which solution and cost is best for them. Because the concept of financial advice online is relatively new, the transition from the existing (invariably face-to-face) model will take time … although it will be quicker than many currently believe.

This situation and knowledge of no one being 'right yet' adds energy to our quest for development. As each solution to the same need advances, we believe the top ten businesses will consolidate or be bought out and will, as other online services have seen, eventually morph into a few large providers across the UK. It could then be argued that 'winning', if this could be judged as such, is not important. What *is* important is being in part of the race from the outset and being both an innovator and a disruptor.

This expected consolidation, possibly after a short term proliferation, is nothing new. A good example is the online aggregators in general insurance, with many larger high profile brands being owned by a few larger banks or insurance companies...and you thought you were shopping around! The economic and regulatory barriers to entry now are high, starting from a relatively low base, but now with significant infrastructure and marketing power. I can't fail to mention the 'soap-suds' wars, as I always do, with their hundreds of products down the supermarket aisles, but only a handful of manufacturers at their core. It almost doesn't matter what you buy, as long as you do buy, because the money will only end up in a small number of corporate bank accounts.

Another vital point is the erosion of value in the product, with the corresponding reduction in future profits. This is almost a 'be careful what you wish for' moment. We, probably unwisely, chuckle at the thought that if our new online offering really took off, we would not be able to cope with the volumes of business it could produce. We aim to avoid the "stack 'em high and sell 'em cheap" approach, although we acknowledge that this too has its merits which we have looked at. But, to get it right based on public or end user choices, what should you do? The answer is to gear up to cope — and we look forward to this journey.

With your planned process in place, check what the competition is doing and *keep* checking; not in order to copy them, but to be aware of their developments and initiatives and, more importantly, why they have chosen the routes they have. Are their choices and options end-user demand led or a concept trial? Are they fishing for additional user interaction or are their choices being directed by interfering 'bean-counters', with innovation taking second place to profit?

Ingenious idea, poorly executed

Is innovation at loggerheads with profit? As an example, there have been some beautiful cars designed over the years, with innovative design or engineering features that have then been throttled in production by cost-cutting, resulting in a very pretty, truly awful vehicle. The original designer would have been embarrassed to put their name on the car. I'm sure you have your own favourite examples of an ingenious idea, poorly executed.

This usually happens when the accountants and 'bean-counters' reduce production costs and quality to make profit from a new idea or model. Robots and automation have helped reduce production costs — but does this cost reduction process apply equally to *online* development and evolution? And is it only restricted to global corporations?

The answer to the latter point is certainly no, which is exciting for entrepreneurs across the globe. Also, I would offer a negative response for the online creativity question. This is because the ability to fantasise about what could be achieved through change, thinking the impossible but not incredible, is essential. The design of such innovations might turn out to be very low cost, and it's no longer the preserve of the large multi-national. Production is a different matter though and this is where you may need to research and seek good advice before even starting.

Can't do Binary

In 1981, I was progressing through a standard comprehensive education. I went to a good school, something I realised only after I'd left, and many parents now pay a premium so that their children can live within its catchment area.

Never the boffin type, daydreaming was more in my line. This was usually in classes other than Art or Engineering Drawing, both of which filled my searching mind with, *"why do they do this as they do?", "could they not do it this way?"* or *"what about if we look at it from a completely different perspective?"* There were no boundaries, which to me was awesome! These subjects actually encouraged random thinking, and passion got you to step out of the sphere you were in and take a completely different look at an opportunity to see if it could be planned, mapped, drawn, administered, delivered in a completely different (and more efficient and exciting) way.

Especially in Art, it was great to see how others in my class had reached different outcomes in the same task. If a subject, such as 'Spatial Progression', was set as a project to paint in oil, the variation of the final pieces was fabulous. Each very different and diverse, explored by searching young minds and then being expressed in paint.

The irony is that this different type of creative thinking was sometimes frowned upon because it was outside the mainstream. But for me, it is exactly that type of thinking that helps me innovate now. As an aside, I thought my own painting was good — but when I saw the work of some of the others over the years, I realised that there might be a better, and more lucrative, future path ahead of me elsewhere.

From an academic perspective, I lacked drive, or interest, in many subjects and had reached puberty where girlfriends were now a real topic, not just imaginary. I had a few dates with a girl called Joan. We were in the same year and in many classes together, including Maths. The Maths curriculum moved on to the subject of Binary and I was immediately stumped. Even now, some thirty-five years later, I have the merest grasp of the concept and like the original lesson it still holds little interest for me, along with the off-side rule in football. Joan teased me with the pet name *"Can't Do Binary"*. It was a fair observation, because I couldn't, but I certainly didn't want everyone to know. A cool young dude, as I preferred to think of myself, needed to remain, well, *cool*.

Our relationship, like the butterfly mentioned previously, got zapped pretty quickly and my world moved on. It is of note that the topic was being taught as standard even then, and subsequently evolved into a subject called Basic, to allow children to do verbalised programming. This has since been replaced by the teaching of coding, which is now being taught to very young children.

Progress? Probably. But still of no interest to me.

That doesn't mean I'm closed to the process and its outcomes. I would prefer to look at concepts, disruption and innovative ways to market, which can then be delivered through an online proposition and, ultimately, coding. The point here is to do what inspires *you*, and let others do the parts that do *not* interest you, playing to your strengths, rather than your shortcomings.

We all have areas of expertise that motivate us. If you work in a small team and need to outsource development, then do. Even if you have someone who is good, but not brilliant, at development, could their skills be used at another junction in the process, whilst contractors build your new structure? We have done this in our own business with great success.

Choose wisely, my friend

If you plan to outsource the development of your new proposition or web development, then choose carefully the provider you use. Whoever is selected must reflect the core message and values you want to send your end user. Above all they must share your passion.

For our alternative new model, we wanted to move away from the traditional older business style and clientele our existing company was used to, preferring to focus on a younger 'Generation X' and the 'Millennial' generation (people born between 1966 and 1980 approximately). We chose the help of a web developer whose staff reflected this age range. This was largely because their attitude, approach and ideas are far removed from our own, older-generation thinking. We needed people above and below the age of forty-three (our own identified age), who had never known a world without computers — as well as people like me, who have had to learn to deal with such innovations over the years. I have to say that the process did not sit comfortably with me at first. However, if we want to engage with our target market, we have to approach them correctly and through the media and communications *they* prefer.

At first, our web developers carefully created a website that met the criteria we had described at several meetings with them. During the early stages of development, what they *thought* we wanted to see turned out not to be what we actually wanted. I asked them to try again, creating the *silliest* website they could think of for the online advice concept we were working on.

Their second response was playful, fun, fresh and fabulous! It reflected an understanding of a new audience for financial services, rather than the traditional model we were specifically trying to avoid for this project. It's not often that you see any of those words related to financial planning, which even at its best is a very dry subject. This was exactly why we needed to break the mould.

It is with some irony that I tell you the statistics from users so far, based on age range, have been defiant of our plans and age expectations, as you can see below:

Demographics/Statistics of visitors to online financial advice website, SaidSo.co.uk

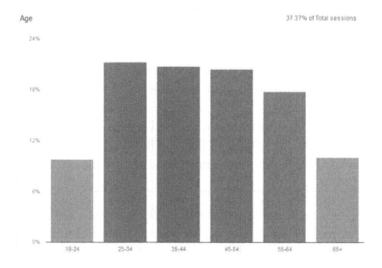

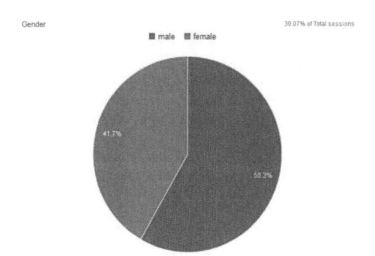

Gender   39.07% of Total sessions

■ male   ■ female

41.7%

58.3%

Technology application for access

Desktop   53.43%

Mobile   35.84%

Tablet   10.73%

(Correct at time of going to press.)

In these statistics so far, the greatest access from a mobile device was via Apple iPhone or iPad — not unsurprising, but it was interesting to see that some had browsed our site using their Xbox.

Source: Chapters Financial Limited / SaidSo.co.uk Analytics / 2015

Even with all our careful planning, brand direction and text tailored to attract 'Millennials', the data in the charts above is a good example of market forces, in letting end users make their own choice as to the services and interaction they have with you.

The internet cannot choose who uses it — but thanks to internet analytics we can allow the end user to indicate their interest in a product or service and be able to see how they view it. Interrogating this data can enable us to develop further initiatives, to meet and even create further demand. When you consider that this is almost the exact opposite of previous marketing orientation — which was marketing-led and focused — this in itself can be seen as a disruption of past sales techniques. Use it to your advantage.

You are always selling yourself; call it what you will

Recently I was both reprimanded and complimented for the same comment. I'd suggested that when we set up our company, we did it with the ambition that 'we never needed to sell anything'. That was probably a bit naïve of us, and a fellow colleague reminded me that we should be under no illusion, we *are* selling ourselves every day of our working lives. It's certainly true that you sell yourself from the first contact to the last, and that our clients and contacts all have a choice which they can exercise easily.

On the other hand, a client suggested they were pleasantly surprised that I had never tried to sell them anything, complimented me on the approach, and then went ahead to make the purchase. Was I selling? Yes, but not in the hard-nosed 'you must buy' way that many people usually loathe.

Selling is not a dirty word, and neither is *profit*, although some might have argued otherwise during the recessionary years. The stabilisation of many of the developed global economies in very recent years has meant that profit can return as the major motivator for corporations, making up for some of the lost gains over the last decade. Global economies are still fragile, that is certain, but they are more informed and connected than ever before — and these almost-instant data sources can in themselves bring some stability because everyone has fair information on what everyone else is up to.

Awkward emotions: do you want to do it anymore?

There is nothing quite like the thrill of starting a business and making it succeed. If you don't get that buzz, then maybe you've been doing it wrong. Or maybe you've been doing it right, just for too long. As the inspiration and early optimism fades, you find yourself wondering if this is still what you wanted.

Do you wake up every morning with a raging desire to push your business onward? Do you go about your routine without a care in the world? Worse than that, do you wake up with fear in your heart because you have to go to work today? You might have had that type of low feeling years ago, which is why you left that place of work to start your own company; so why is it back now? I don't mean the day-to-day problems that we all face. I am referring to the real underlying sense that this is not where you want to be, and if it doesn't give a bit, you may have to hit the metaphorical 'eject' button. *Don't!* You are on the right lines and it's a case of holding your nerve.

We all usually feel frustration when faced with the same-old, same-old. Routine is a great framework to build a reliable and solid business where everyone — you, your staff, customers and enquirers — has a fair idea of what the experience of dealing with your business will feel like. Having a steady pair of hands is great... but possibly boring, especially if you've been blessed with the entrepreneurial spirit that caused you to start the business in the first place.

If you are going to start a new project, it is important to know where you are in your own world, business, team and mind. Once you have that straight you can apply and manage the energy, both good and bad, that will be needed to disrupt current thinking and deliver new concepts.

Finding renewed love... for your business

Have you looked back at the reasons why you started your business in the first place, both positive and negative? I took nine months to lay out all the detailed plans of our new business launch and I still kept the notes after pressing the 'go' button. It's been a whirlwind since then and you too may be finding it hard to keep your feet on the ground. The business you've created is always hungry for your attention and time, and almost seems to keep you away from the business you actually want to conduct.

Well, take control again. The reality is that those original notes will probably clutter up some cupboard for years to come. However, on the odd occasion, they are worth dusting off, both to chuckle at how you saw it then and the reality of what the enterprise has since become. More importantly, they allow you to relive some of the emotions that you went through during your planning and to feel once more the energy that you had when making such inspired choices.

The 'fine line'

Your business may be running along just fine and there is some harmony inherent in a "don't fix what isn't broken" attitude. I have mentioned that I studied art and oil painting. My own paintings were adequate, but there was always a fine line between something being fresh and finished, and producing a piece that was overdone and overworked. This can happen when you write a book, or do anything creative, and that includes innovating in a business.

Our new online model project was launched and we have continued to develop it over the first year. We are very pleased with both the launch and the subsequent updates and changes, keeping fresh and vibrant. However, we'd reached a line at the time of writing this book. We're launching some updates, and then we're going to leave it alone, say for six months, to let it all bed in. In our opinion, there is a greater risk of detracting than adding benefit by more additions. That's our current take on the 'fine line'.

The art of the possible

Continuing the 'art' theme, there is an art in making things happen in an innovative way.

The key components to your strategy may be to look at what has gone before, see what assets you have now, estimate the potential distance you can go and imagine what else you could achieve with what you have. In this case you will need to do some real free thinking, applying the art of the possible.

In a way, it's a bit like the art classes I attended all those decades ago: taking a subject, taking up the assets of paper and paint, and seeing where your imagination could take you. And then having the ability to show this to others whom you trust to ask, if you feel you have lost direction, where *they* think they would go next.

Unforeseen consequences

When's the last time you said: *'Wow'*?

Usually it's a positive term, but when was the last time you said it when you looked at the unforeseen consequences of a process or innovation? The one that made you stop and think, *Wow! If you do that you could also do... which would mean that you could... which means that you could cut costs/improve productivity/increase distribution/create a completely different application to the route the process had originally planned*? Not just a rinse and repeat of what you're already doing, just like everyone else, but a genuine innovation that you didn't see coming.

It's probably the same project that the 'energy zapper' types turned their noses up at, the people who are far from positive about free thinking when working on a concept or project, and who seek only to stop it. This is nothing new, as history demonstrates:

Things move along so rapidly nowadays that people saying: "It can't be done," are always being interrupted by somebody doing it.

This quotation is noted as 1903 in the American publication, *Puck*. However, there are those who argue it dates much earlier, possibly even to Confucius.

I often hear business managers and owners say to their staff that the door is open for anyone to bring their problems to their desk... as long as they also bring possible solutions with them. The resulting conversations are far more positive when there's an option or two to resolve a problem or opportunity.

Whatever you do, keep an open mind. If you have never had this 'wow' experience, then you need to find one. They are wonderful, and they are out there waiting for you to discover. A success may prove not to be innovation at all.

Never fear failure. You've heard it before: you can't expect to get it right all the time, especially when you are trying to disrupt existing models and plans. Franklin D Roosevelt noted in his inaugural speech in 1933 that *"There is nothing to fear but fear itself"*. It is of note that he was elected at a time when his country was in the grip of the Great Depression. This statement may have been a calming influence: —

"So, first of all, let me assert my firm belief that the only thing we have to fear is... fear itself — nameless, unreasoning, unjustified terror which paralyzes needed efforts to convert retreat into advance. In every dark hour of our national life a leadership of frankness and of vigor has met with that understanding and support of the people themselves which is essential to victory. And I am convinced that you will again give that support to leadership in these critical days."

Those were great words at a time of change, uncertainty and blind faith in the future. A bit like business disruption really! It is of note that these words could also be relevant to the surprise EU Referendum result in the UK. You might argue that in the innovation process of delivery, it is better to be a fundamental failure than an average success. An 'average' success may prove not to be innovation at all.

Barristers warned not to store confidential information in the Cloud

Thinking of unforeseen consequences, and bringing this topic up-to-date, the publication *City A.M.* reported in late February 2016 that The Bar Council in the UK has warned barristers that in their adoption of Cloud technology and storage, the US authorities might use their own legislation to access data stored there, without permission. This is applicable to Cloud or external backup services owned by US companies, even if the data itself is subject to legal privilege in the UK. It could mean in principle that the barrister could have breached the UK's Data Protection Act if data were accessed to gather confidential information. The likelihood of any of us, professionals or otherwise, checking a Cloud contract for US data issues is unlikely; even if you did see it, we would struggle to recognise it as a risk in such terms.

As a small business carrying personal client information, we have not adopted Cloud technology for similar reasons. We have not seen the Cloud have a major fail yet, and we will be interested to see what this looks like if it happens. We will also be interested to see what the repercussions are and the way they are handled, so we can make a decision about whether this widely-adopted technical innovation and its evolution suits our business. We appreciate that the costs of buying and replacing our own servers is expensive, but it does allow us to maintain security of data, and this is as vital to our main business as it is to our new offering.

Time is money... it really is

We experienced a significant management issue with a trademark some time back. It was challenging, protracted and time consuming. The outcome was sufficient to allow us to move forward.

Personally, I thought that the other directors and I had done well to achieve the outcome we did, without (so we thought) being distracted from the main business. Some two years later, I was speaking to a close contact who, without hesitation, said about that time and situation: *"Well, you were extremely distracted at the time,"* in the context of the stifled progress we had made over the intervening period. My retort was immediate, almost like the pantomime in suggesting *"oh no we weren't..."* and then I stopped myself. With hindsight I could see that I was wrong and that their observation was entirely correct. We *had* been distracted; hugely so. Yes, we came out the other side, but the time lost, the capacity for thinking, for management, for production, for direction, had been consumed by that case. To say we won the battle and lost the war would be too extreme, but the sentiment is fair. Had we genuinely focused our energy on the business, and limited our time where possible on the challenge, we would have been further forward by now.

'Time is money' as they say. Money can be lost and regained. Time cannot. Be careful where you direct your personal energy, because it can only be spent once and it is then lost forever. Make it pay!

Proof of concept

Have you reached the 'fine line' with your business? To some extent, we have with our main business. There's always some housekeeping and tuning to be done — but it's not broken, quite the reverse, and it does not need fixing. To some extent it's not greatly challenging either.

Workloads get volumes through, which creates challenges, but invariably it's not greatly challenging work. And to be clear, I like a challenge. What about you?

The economist and political scientist Joseph Schumpeter observed in the early part of the twentieth century that invention is the exercise of the creative impulse. It should be noted that that a creative impulse may be of limited use if it is not delivered through the second stage, innovation. The *innovation* is the part that will provide the rewards.

Joseph Schumpeter popularised the term 'creative destruction' in economics, which is not surprising, given that the economic period he worked through was the Great Depression. It is suggested that he was the first scholar to theorise about entrepreneurship, identifying innovation as a critical dimension of economic change. In particular, he observed that technological innovation often creates temporary monopolies, allowing abnormal profits that are soon competed away by rivals and imitators. These temporary monopolies are necessary to provide the incentive for firms to develop new products and processes.

It was reported on the website AEI.org how the Theory of Creative Destruction is relevant to today's business, including comments on the Netflix Effect of August 2015. The article and study by scholar at AEI, Mark Perry, professor of economics and finance at The University of Michigan (August 2015), entitled *The 'Netflix Effect': An Excellent Example of 'Creative Destruction'* considers the power of this process and its impact on existing industries, which it indicates have been 'Netflixed'.

From our own business plans, our creative thinking was to replicate the delivery of our proposition, in a streamlined form, like a traditional business but purely online. Our aim: proof of concept. Our motivator? Partly fuelled by ego, partly by pride, I want to be known as the father of online financial advice. Partly greed, because if it works, I can sell it. And finally, by a bit of fear in the fact that I can do this, I am reaching fifty years old in a year or so, I am full of energy right now and if I don't see this through with the business wisdom I have, I will regret it in years to come.

I must admit to having quite a lot of emotion running through me when I wrote that last paragraph, however this then led to desire, gumption, passion, even thirst to continue to achieve. And whilst this remains with me, I will grab it!

With the wisdom of business processes behind you, starting a new business or concept is not daunting. However, like the first business that cost you sleepless nights years ago, any new enterprise needs a motivator. This time round, I am sure the motivator is going to be different to the first and may not be without risk; but it originates from a position of greater strength in terms of both knowledge and finance.

All the same, I hope it is just as challenging. If not, you might want to flag this as a query: do you believe you can go further than the initial plan? Otherwise, the outcome you achieve may not have been worth the effort. It's got to have a key selling point that is going to move it, and your existing main business, forward — or else be neutral to it — to be worth the energy and focus it will require from you.

My own greatest fear was the distraction from the main business. Our careful planning avoided this and it is always something to be watched. You can be the master of each enterprise as long as you concentrate.

Be careful what you wish for; you just might get it

Have you ever thought that you might have massively underestimated how far a plan or concept could go? If it could reach even 10% of the dream you have just conjured up in your mind, could you and the infrastructure you have around you meet the demand?

This would obviously be a great problem to have and perhaps a massive headache. Plan and pitch your business plans at the level your intuition, and market research, lead you — and allow space for evolution to move even more quickly than you dreamed.

Modernisation

If innovation is not for you — and you know it will require a lot of energy and focus — then you will also be aware that the world moves on and your existing business will need to reflect this. Is a modernisation programme in order, to move your business forward into the next decade?

Standing still is not an effective option if you want to remain profitable into the future. Feel free to disagree with this statement, but it is my experience that the business headwinds you will face may make your current rituals ineffective in a short time. I am not sorry to make the challenge that, in my mind, standing still is the same as gradually moving backwards. It's like a business inflation factor that ebbs at your expense.

Modernisation and business evolution must be embraced. An alternative is to be swallowed by a consolidator who snaps up your business for a fraction of its real value and modernises it, probably without you. This may suit you if you've reached your natural end point. However, I would guess that the fact you are reading this book means you probably haven't.

And for the other fifty years?

I would challenge you also. If your chosen vocation has reached a natural plateau, to think about what else you could do to diversify other aspects of your life. I have recently met middle working-age people who, as employees in a pay scale, have reached the top level of their career at a relatively young age - and by this I mean age forty-ish. I appreciate that this statement alone might be ageist, especially taking into account that in the current ageing UK demographic the likelihood of living another fifty years, to age ninety, is not unreasonable. Looking for an alternative rather than accepting your lot, possibly dictated by someone else's outdated opinion of how a career scale should constrain your career, is always worthwhile. One individual I spoke to had started to invest surplus funds into longer term investments, mainly because the company pension scheme would not give them a realistic standard of living at sixty-six or more.

Having two careers during a working lifetime is not uncommon in current times. I think this option has only come to reality in the last two decades, possibly a reflection of economic times and the extension of longevity across UK and other developed nations. Crossover, with both careers running at the same time, is not uncommon either — and in fact it's a growing trend. This is innovation and disruption but on a personal scale. I applaud it.

Whatever you decide to do, take time out to stop at junctions in your life to see where you are going and to check that it is the path that you, your partner, family, desire and want to take. You only get one life, just make sure you live it.

Nimble on your feet

In 2016, I called a large insurance company for some documentation for a client's arrangements. We needed to make changes to their plan and wanted to get organised accordingly. Even in this first sentence, I can hear you asking: 'What, you had to *call* them? Why did you do that? Did you not think about going *online*?' You might guess that the company concerned was long established. Although it portrays itself as progressive, with Apps for this, and online for that, the reality is that if you have a historic policy or arrangement with them then you are plunged into the dark ages of telephone and paper.

The lady was very helpful and accommodating as I requested an email of the documents and her last words to me were: 'I will order those for you now and we will email them over to you no later than 16th February'. All of which fine, until you realise that the 16th February in this case was a full *twenty days* hence. Twenty days… for an *email*! Now, this is not a rant about poor service or even poor service times; however, it is an observation of opportunity.

I think it's a real-life, small, even 'tip of the iceberg' example, of a large industry leader being weighed down by the business legacy of its own past. Everything it achieved decades ago is now an administrative weight on the business as it tries to secure new business without being bogged down by the old business.

One possible way round this could be to segregate old and new businesses, with innovation being applied to the new business and containment being applied to the old.

'Legacy lag' for established and usually large businesses has been affecting businesses for decades. This is why small businesses can be so nimble, providing the opportunity to work profitably around and through such lumbering institutions.

Examples might be banks, with their pass-the-parcel of debt problems; nuclear fuel once a generation plant is decommissioned; even vehicle manufacturers with the emission test scandals that will see millions wiped off profits both now and for years to come. The problems are clear and usually headline grabbing; the way these issues, even crises, are handled and managed will decide whether a company continues to operate or goes bust. Many of these larger companies with legacy business are unable either through desire or understandably, profitability, to adjust the old model to new methods.

What a great opportunity to disrupt!

Scared of something different

Chapter Three: Innovation

Innovation: *a new method, idea, product, etc.*

It's fun to innovate. There are no rules for a start — which, coming from a heavily regulated financial services background, is a relief! Although it may seem unwieldy and without structure, you do have a blank page in which to create a structure that others will use, will possibly plagiarise and will follow in times to come. So don't be shy in your early adoption of the concept; as you move through *creation* to *innovation*, make sure that it all suits you, your business, your needs and objectives and your profit expectations when the expected higher volumes eventually flow.

You will start to see a path to success, as follows: —

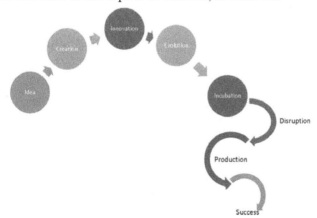

The lines for each phase are not clearly visible in advance. Each phase needs to be discovered, developed and nurtured... by you.

Innovation, in my opinion, cannot exist without evolution. The definition of evolution is *the gradual development of something.* I am not sure about the 'gradual' part of this saying, although the underlying sentiment is sound enough. In these revolutionary times, technology blurs the lines of what can be achieved and can allow old approaches to be challenged, even shredded and re-developed, rather than gradually advanced. Inconceivable as an opportunity only a decade ago, the real opportunity for many businesses to be turned on their heads and be re-invented in many ways, particularly distribution, is very exciting.

Be careful that the innovation that you perceive is not just artificial product differentiation, but real innovation. This can take the form of a re-discovery or re-birth of an old concept, turning it into something entirely new, producing truly exciting outcomes. When is the last time you thought of your business as racy or sexy? This is your opportunity to make it so.

Innovator or Disruptor? Both are good

It has been fascinating to watch real innovators as they disrupt existing established markets through the use of technology. The disruption itself is not the fascinating part, although it has its moments; it's the concept of approaching existing markets in completely different ways which invariably brings new vibrancy to a market that was getting stale, or at least complacent and in need of a good shake-up. The reaction of existing market makers to the interlopers is also worthy of note: they may combat the entry with alternative offerings, price reductions and often simple ridicule. However, they behave in this way to their cost. In piping up they merely draw more attention to the new offerings, than to their own existing product offering. Sometimes no reaction is the best reaction.

Higher profile online examples might be Purplebricks. com in the residential property market and, of course, Über for city taxi services. There are many others, such as Ocado for grocery shopping — each providing an alternative proposition to the norm (which had been set in pre-recession times) and usually solely achieved by the application of technology to a situation. The innovation is simply a matter of applying new thinking to an existing market, proposition or opportunity.

Will these innovations stand the test of time? Probably; and they too will evolve over time as technology applications improve still further, and eroding the market share of those existing operators who do not embrace change at its present rapid rate. Personally, I am not normally an advocate of early adoption of disruptive change, preferring to leave that to those better versed on that topic. In this new Fourth Industrial Revolution era we tend to be one of the first to market, disrupting wherever we can to extend our existing service digitally to a national audience with a low cost, simplified online service. This is called **SaidSo.co.uk**. We are a small and admittedly very dynamic micro-company. If we can do it, why can't you?

I am not suggesting that you should shake the living daylights out of your industry or profession just for the sake of it. More importantly, I am not suggesting that you junk your existing business that you have fought so hard to create, only to reinvent it online. It's a lot subtler than that. But if it could be done, at the very least you need to be ready for the new entrant who is probably already working on a digital model that can be delivered nationally, on your doorstep, at lower cost and with higher profit margins. Are you ready?

Neither am I advocating a straightforward upgrade of your existing e-commerce systems. E-commerce is nothing new, although their deliveries (such as touch-pay systems where suitable) are different. What I *am* recommending is that you take all the experience and ingenuity you have learned during the development of your business, and send it all back to the drawing board. Do it alone, or with trusted individuals who share your passion, to renew, research and develop further.

No respecter

New entrants may emerge from obvious quarters, such as the existing profession, trade or industry. Be assured, *someone* will try (possibly not an acknowledged player), someone who has distribution channels and can see a path to profit in the short or medium term. The internet and technology are no respecter of boundaries, such as experience. Indeed, those that hold distribution capabilities through physical networks, or even social media, telecommunications and the like, may be able to enter the market simply because they have more access to users and the internet offers them a low cost entry point to an online solution.

Options to disrupt

With my colleagues, I run a small financial planning company, offering a traditional face-to-face advice model on a fee basis from a High Street premises. All fairly conventional fare, but it has its limitations, with most business being transacted within a thirty-mile radius. We moved to a fee-based model in 2007 because of our view that commission alternatives were going to disappear, and this proved to be a stabilising move for our business income streams. To some extent, this also proved to be a key selling point in its own right at that time, although all our competitors have moved to this profile because of new legislation some five years later.

I would like to have said that it was a unique selling point — however, a limited few of our competitors had also taken the leap into this new territory. Our early adoption of the alternative process put the mainstream competition on the back foot, at the same time as it accelerated our income because of our business experience in using the fee-based and transparent system, which it turned out that many clients preferred. It was not easy at the time. On many occasions, we as a management team questioned our logic. However, standing by the agreed plan saw us through the deep economic recession that soon followed, as we majored on service rather than on sales and initial commission.

There are some limitations to this traditional, High Street based offering. As an example, you might guess that the model mainly attracts local people, usually within the county or London.

Also, it tends to attract a more mature, older age group who prefer the personal approach to our professional services model. By older, I mean people over fifty-five who prefer to avoid internet transactions when it comes to their own money. This is a sweeping statement and I know it will attract the scorn of those in the same age group who read this and do *all* their money planning online. It's one of those occasions when I would be very happy to be proved wrong!

However, we have experienced that people under the age of forty tend to prefer to avoid or simply do not take face-to-face advice, often undertaking their own research or using online alternatives.

To attract additional market users, some of our competitors are looking at (and in some cases already running) online services in the following formats:

- Skype interview and advice;

- Video conferencing interview and advice;

- Robo-Advice (effectively no human interaction, just algorithms to provide a computer solution to a client's needs);

- Online financial advice (a mixture of digital input, human advice and digital returns). We affectionately call this Remote Online Advice using both human and tech power, or ROMO advice for short; (see Saidso. co.uk).

- A mixture of the above.

You can see from these examples that each market offering provides the same effective outcome; it's just that the way that it provides a solution is different. And which works the best? No one knows yet but each will evolve their own proposition as the public use, and approve or otherwise, the service. The public will decide.

Also, you should look abroad for alternatives, and at what has and has not worked in your business line. When doing so, look first to the USA where their transition to the integration of tech in most areas is already well advanced. However, this is not always the case; many UK and European companies are leading the way in their field. One clear example of this is the building of global 5G communications in Surrey.

It is not unsurprising to see there are different ideas about the way into new markets... and the future... and you may be able to apply the same principles to your existing business. I hope you are feeling inspired by the prospect rather than weary at the thought. Shaking the existing model to see what opportunities fall out is always worthwhile. I have spoken to many business owners who have discovered a profitable business line as a consequence of winning another contract to which the new line or service was only one part of the project. They have interrogated this area and then offered it as a business service to other companies and users, to extend out the new profit point. The new line or opportunity has been a by-product of the original concept.

I spoke to one company that took in part-finished goods, packaged them and then distributed the end product to consumers. They had not done the packaging part before and had to invest in infrastructure to win the overall contract. However, they then found through their management information data that the packaging element of the programme was more profitable than the balance of the contract, which would normally have been their core business objective. They now actively seek packaging opportunities to add value into their main business.

You could quite fairly argue that this is not innovation, rather a journey of discovery of what else they could achieve with the current infrastructure. However, the ability to move into a space that they had not occupied before, through disrupting their standard thinking to make it work, to then recognise its profitability and to then actively seek out this new revenue stream, is not to be ignored.

Importantly, the positive attitude of *"let's get this working"* in this example is a testament to the change curve in making it happen.

The *Sunday Times* (2016) recently quoted Mark Fields, the US CEO of Ford, saying of automated cars: *"Everyone is talking about Silicon Valley disrupting the car business. We are going to disrupt ourselves."*

So, if you could disrupt your own business, delivering the proposition online and remotely to the end user, whatever business you are in, *which* offering would you prefer to use, receive, proffer? Remember that to some extent you may be competing against yourself. Therefore (as we have done) keep the new entity separate from your main brand to begin with. I think it is good to revisit the attributes of the existing business, its key selling points — if not entirely unique now — and the original ones that made you start the business in the first place. When was the last time you revisited these key building blocks to see if they still held water in the vastly more interconnected world that we now live in?

Infancy

Around a decade ago, Twitter was newly established and Facebook was just becoming well-known. It is astonishing to realise how these social media offerings have changed the world forever for millions of people. Events across the world are tweeted instantly, often before the news media can get hold of them, detailing every conceivable action. I appreciate that some people hate it — and that's up to them — but it *is* the future.

Mobile connectivity is being improved with 4G telecommunications; 5G is also now being developed and built for release in a few years' time, bringing us all a lot closer together. Wearable tech is on my wrist as I type these words, and these advances will only cease when the human mind reaches its limits of new thinking... which won't be any time soon.

What's more, I don't think we have even got started yet! The world has changed dramatically in the last decade, both in terms of technology, its distribution and innovation, but also in terms of business acumen. You know this; you have already survived the deepest recession for nearly a century and you are still here, as is your business.

But, just like social media, you've made it through your infancy phase and now it's time to move through the awkward growth years. I am sure the age of your plans may have been extended because of the last recession and its challenges. But now is the time to make change and you're going to need to plan first.

Coming to a High Street near you?

How about taking a journey of potential change with me? I was thinking about something that we all know, that most of us have used on a regular basis, and that we probably take for granted. I thought about your local High Street, with its bars, retail shops and coffee shops, travel agents and estate agents, all ready to serve you as soon as you walk in.

Usually bustling, especially at the weekend, there was once a thought that its future was doomed because of online shopping. Some three years ago in my last book, *The Recession is Over, Time to Grow*, I looked at this issue. I came to the view that the 'real' shop *will* survive, but it would have to evolve significantly to remain an important part of our lives. I observed the growth of 'brick and click', where you might visit a store, browse their offerings and then buy online, probably from your phone, and have your purchase delivered direct to your home. There was nothing really revolutionary in those comments, other than to confirm that, three years later, this is now commonplace.

So, what next? Here are some more examples of consumer-based tech changes that will evolve further:-

Some car dealers are now selling cars from deluxe but somewhat smaller showrooms because... *they have no(or few) cars in them* (for example: Audi, Digital Showroom, City, London). Using touch-sensitive screens and interactive concepts to model the car and choices to your heart's desire, you can 'experience' before you buy.

Audi is not alone in this type of change. Hyundai introduced its Rockar store concept in Kent: retail shops with no sales people, to keep, I believe, the 'interference' between buyer and maker to a minimum.

One High Street and online retailer has introduced same-day delivery for orders placed. Argos, I believe, is the first of the major retailers to do this. They won't be the last.

There's no missing the fact that 4G telecommunications are becoming widely available. Shops can now fit iBeacons to their windows to pump messages to your smart phone or wearable tech (watch, jacket, glasses) if that is your preference, to tell you of today's, or even this hour's, special offer and make you stop and visit. It might be anything from 10% off the price, to a free muffin with your Latte. It's not widespread in the UK yet, but give it time. Many town centres are offering Wi-Fi across their area to maintain visitor numbers because people see this as a standard, rather than a luxury.

I thought the concept of tech-based spectacles was good. I had planned to buy some before they were suddenly removed from sale by the manufacturers. Looking at this decision further, it seems that this withdrawal didn't happen because the product was not good. It seems that it was. It was just not *great*. And with this margin still there, the strongest possible decision was taken — to withdraw, at least for the time being. I have no doubt that this communication and connectivity solution will return to the market and I look forward to it.

Remote SIM communication will soon be built into every electronic product you buy and can be integrated to your personal communicator, so that you can turn the heating on, and the kettle on, view what's in the fridge for tea tonight, and of course get the oven warming so that everything in your home is set perfectly for you before you walk in the door.

I understand that the market for personal SIM cards and smartphone market is reaching saturation point. This is exampled by the Androidauthority.com website on the Chinese market in May 2015. This does not mean that the consumer experience cannot be enhanced. However, with most of us having two or three SIMs (Subscriber Identity Modules) — say in your phone, tablet and other device — the benefit in our having any more is probably limited. But this does not stop the everyday /household devices that we use from having SIM communication facilities so that we can control them remotely from our mobile device. The scope for this growth is enormous.

Nokia, in its document, FutureWorks 5G use cases and requirements (2014) notes:

Data will be one of the key drivers for 5G and in new parts of this system we may for the first time see no dedicated voice service – in 5G, voice is expected to be handled as an application, simply using the data connectivity provided by the communication system. Data is growing at a rate between 25% and 50% annually and is expected to continue towards 2030.

Could *you* use this growth with your product to diversify its appeal?

5G telecommunications will be a quantum leap forward again. I wonder if 4G will become the poor relative of the data rollouts, with many people possibly switching straight from 3G to 5G telecommunications. And will the 5G initiative rewrite what we already have on our phones, such as Apps? The part I find exciting about the possible death of the App is that those who build and produce them will not allow this to happen. They will just adapt and disrupt, to increase their relevance in a highly evolutionary industry.

So, what does this mean for your High Street?

No one knows, but the reality could be no stockrooms required, for example, with stores becoming smaller and only requiring the frontage of a shop rather than 'real' facilities. Full length scanners can now measure your body height, size and measurements; perfect for getting the right sizes for your needs. Imagine: stores maintaining your details and measurements. You build your clothing requirements from their range, while they give you on-screen visuals of how you will look, if not feel, having enticed you into the shop with a special offer from their iBeacon. Obviously there is no need to carry your purchases home, having paid from your phone, because these will be delivered later.

Next door is a new car showroom in what used to be a mobile phone shop. The temptation to try the latest sports model is compelling, especially with no salespeople. The car is obviously fully compatible with your phone, for more than just calls; it also knows your driving style and preferences and will probably 'test-drive' them for you to check that you are appropriately matched.

There's a staff member on hand in case you get stuck, but there's no need for a whole sales team. Obviously, no cash transactions take place, with the assistant accepting touch-pay options to their tablet as they move around the retail facility. There is no longer a till as such; although the option to pay by Bitcoin has not gained traction yet. However, you can pay in any other real currency, accessed by biometric banking security systems on your touch phone. You can even pay with Euros following the negotiated exit of Great Britain from the Eurozone after the close-fought leave vote in the shocking 2016 EU Referendum. It's true that the predictions for *financial technology*, or 'fintech' for short, are endless. The possibilities are endless as well.

The back of the retail store, where the stockroom and staff catering area used to be, has been divided and sold off for residential accommodation. This is much to the annoyance of the local council, whose council tax income has fallen with the loss of demand for this prime land.

Parking is so much easier than it used to be. With space availability and booking on your phone, it's never been easier to park close to where you want to be, or indeed to recharge your car's fuel cells whilst in town.

Are you daydreaming of what could be with you soon? But anything is possible.

This demonstrates there are no limits to what could be achieved without seriously changing the main point — in this case 'going shopping'. The only limitations are technology and human thinking. Will there come a time when 3D printers are outdated by 4D printers? What might the 4th dimension be? Time, perhaps, but let's see what's offered.

Rather than 'click and collect' or 'brick and click' principles, will you one day go into town and 'click and print' your product there and then? Or will you buy in store or online, at your home PC (if these still exist) or through your phone, and the product you've bought be printed out for you at home? Far-fetched? Perhaps utility rooms in houses will be turned into print rooms, where all your household goods turn up, freshly made and still warm from production, at the instruction of your phone.

The future of Apps... or Wapps?

I know, when I look on my mobile phone or tablet, that there are lots of Apps installed, several screens full in fact. And yes, I know you can group them, but then I find I forget them! Perhaps this is because they do not engage me enough at the outset, usually being selected by subject and the views and reviews of others indicated by their star rating. Many were downloaded months or even years ago, on the assumption that they would prove useful, only ever to be used once. And like many people, I have never got round to uninstalling them.

Is this the beginning of personal data overload? If I now visit either the App Store or Google Play, I am bombarded by new Apps, many of them reportedly doing the same thing, just in a new variant. Persuaded accordingly, I download a new one — only to find a better one a few months later, and soon my device is full of useless Apps! Is this progress?

I can understand the long term marketing motivation for 'shop store' Apps, as it ties you in to their brand. Brand loyalty is vital to future business success. I find some of the games, and their ever improving graphics (both in game and in device), great for passing the time waiting for a train.

The transition to the extension of a business proposition as an App adds greater complication and opportunity in gaining longer-term end user engagement and brand loyalty. Having said that, I have struggled to see the business proposition of why I should put out the likes of 'SaidSo', our online financial advice website, as an App. As part of our ongoing progression, the website was created in a mobile-friendly way, to marry in with Google's preference towards mobile-friendly sites for the optimisation of their search engine. We appreciate that Google changes its stance regularly, and that's what keeps them fresh... and ahead! Any SaidSo.co.uk App, we believe, would be lost wherever you go to find your Apps from. And if you were trying to input financial data you certainly would want a larger screen (probably not recommended in a crowded space) than is available on your watch or wearable tech.

Like most technology applications in their infancy, the App world is going to be shaken soon by the likes of Google who have started to look at how to disrupt the App community, with their new App-streaming model (possibly a web of Apps/ or "Wapps" for short, a Google App search facility), which is still in the build phase and due to be released in the next few years. It should allow the user to view content from an App without having the App installed on their device; the content seen in the browser would look and feel like the App, however without needing to install it.

This suggests a solution to compatibility issues between different types of App. Some of the newer phones use a low frequency Bluetooth application. This can mean that the App from your fitness monitor, as an example, does not connect with your mobile device. As you can see, there is plenty of scope to innovate and disrupt.

With many of us now mainly using the social media Apps, for the time being anyway, the way we access information is changing. Therefore, if an App can translate and evolve its application further to, amongst other things, wearable technology, its future may be brighter than initially thought. This new opportunity may attract us to the market for our current online business proposition, especially to help with brand awareness and loyalty. Only time will tell whether Apps survive in their current format or will we be browsing "Wapps"?

The challenge to the App industry is exciting as they are prompted to innovate.

Tools of the trade

One institution that has tools that can change outcomes in the future is the Bank of England. One obvious tool at its disposal is interest rates. People may be aware of change because it pushes the cost of their mortgage up or down, or savings interest negative or positive, but they may not see it as a tool to control *personal spending*, which it is. Every month (although this is about to be reduced to eight times per annum) the news reports the Bank's latest views on the UK economy in the context of the global economy, and why it has (usually) decided to leave alone or move their base rate accordingly. It has a range of such tools, some less obvious than others. One that has come to prevalence since the economic crisis of 2008 is quantitative easing, the modern description of which is: —

"An unconventional form of monetary policy where a Central Bank creates new money electronically to buy financial assets, like government bonds. This process aims to directly increase private sector spending in the economy and return inflation to target."

Whichever tools the Bank of England chooses, the real outcome of the changes they make takes time. Normally about two years will elapse before the full effects of policy changes are felt in the economy, and for the aspect of the economy the Governor and committee has targeted to respond positively. The concept of controlling the flow of money and trade through an economy is nothing new.

"Money is, above all, a subtle device
for linking the present to the future."
— John Maynard Keynes 1883-1920, *Hopes Betrayed*

But also his colleague Alfred Marshall on the value of gold and silver in 1887 explained: —

"It would act at once on Lombard Street, and make people inclined to lend more; it would swell deposits and book credits and so enable people to increase their speculation with borrowed capital; it would therefore increase the demand for commodities and so raise prices... It would have the ultimate effect of adding to the volume of currency required for circulation, as I think, because prices having risen, a person who found it answer to his purpose to have an average of £17 in currency in his pocket would now require £18 or £19; and so on for others..."

We have already noted in this book that sometimes the answer is behind you. It is ironic that having been through a significant period of quantitative easing with money throughout the developed nations, Marshall refers to a similar process with the Royal Commission about the quantity of gold lowering the value of the currency concerned. With this historic principle noted, I wondered if we will be referring to this text in a hundred years' time, but with the use of Bitcoin or some other electronic currency style, and shaking with mirth at the outdated currency of the early twenty-first century that was money. The monetary vehicle has changed, but not the concept. With the introduction of plastic notes in the UK in 2016, real money may last for a little while longer!

Lags and separation

Time lag is an important factor for innovative thinking. Too slow and you can be overtaken; too fast and the public may not be ready to take the next step you are proposing. We certainly experienced that a decade ago in the UK retail online financial advice market. The timing was too early, the public unready as trust in the internet had yet to grow over the intervening years, and the product offering was a failure. It's great to write that word, "failure". Not because of the word itself — but I'm glad with hindsight that the fear of it did not stop us from continuing and, of course, learning.

From innovation comes *evolution and development*, which provides *experience*, which then creates *product*, and so on. There has to be an element of market timing for delivery, and your end-user research may suggest the appropriate timing, with a suitable marketing programme. It is important that you control any time lag and its key project elements to meet your planned objectives at the pre-launch, launch and growth phases. You will intrigue your competitors, but you should stay continually alert for their replications. They may have some 'useful' ideas, but be careful not to plagiarise those.

We still think that our online concept is too early for the UK public to engage with fully and naturally. However, we believe its time is coming, and our brand is gaining depth and recognition in the process. Whatever happens, as suggested earlier, you need to be in the game and that is all about timing.

Degrees of separation

Our failures in the early attempts at our new concept were valuable for the learning and intellectual property they provided. What worked, what didn't, what added value for the end user, what just ticked regulatory boxes? The process of making a small detail change that creates a completely different outcome is vital. In a way, a miss is as good as a mile — but in reverse.

Look both ways, look all ways

Do not underestimate attention to detail; your end-user certainly won't. Visuals, spelling, graphics, quality, connectivity all have to be aligned with the product thinking. If this level of minutiae is not your forte, get someone who relishes detail to do it for you. At every junction of creativity look both ways, look all ways. If you were to point one element in a different direction, would it give you a better outcome? If you don't know, build two, three, ten models and then take what's best from each to create *the* version you want to represent the wonderful disruption you want to display.

We did exactly this over a period of time and I cannot advocate the value of this strategy highly enough. It's like wandering into an ideas cupboard, viewable only by the team, and picking off the premium quality thinking to add to your recipe.

Regulators controlling real innovation, even progress?

I recently undertook a transaction with a financial services firm, using a new — and to them, innovative — service. Overall, the experience was a step forward but it felt laboured by the time it was complete. The video conference was held in the branch, because they could not achieve it any other compliant way, and it was clumsy. The appointment itself was confirmed by text message.

It was interesting to experience the process as an end-user (direct to client). However, while I observed the regulatory boxes being ticked while the process plodded along, I began to question whose benefit all this was for. As a veteran of the industry I could see what was being achieved. I had the desire to gain the end product but also felt that the process was not for me, or even for them, but was there mainly to demonstrate to a regulator in an audit process that everything had been confirmed to me, the client, before I took any action. The staff member was able to print documents on the printer in the room for me, and a scanner was on hand if I needed to give them a copy of anything requested in advance.

I certainly felt 'complied' in a regulatory sense, but in no way engaged. This was the first of three phases, each of them taking place in the branch, and each taking about forty-five minutes. If I had not been a confident internet user, however, I might have found this approach more comforting, especially when dealing with money. This seems to me to challenge the assumption that everyone is comfortable divulging any sensitive information online and remotely. I believe this is on its way; we would not have innovated otherwise. However, there may be a human 'lag' between technology progression and the end-user's willingness to use these new facilities.

As an additional point, and to slightly contradict the last notes, we have experienced the power of 'free'. With the introduction of a free facility download from our new service offering, the real personal information provided to get the free offer has been enlightening.

You can guess that speed, end-user convenience or real innovation did not score highly in this video conference example. In reality, it was already-outdated tech that was being deployed to increase distribution at low cost. This has its place for a limited time span. It was this aspect that made me feel that, for a well-established household name to make such changes, was innovation indeed. But it was still a slow progress and was already behind the times.

I can't say I was inspired! We had previously gone up against this same organisation in an awards category — and now we understood why they had not won.

As suggested before, no one has the single perfect answer. 'The answer' is probably a combination of answers; it's just a question of which ones. My greatest concern was, in this instance, the interference and limited real value of regulation. No advice was given at the first meeting, which was effectively a fact finding process. So, why was it so long and cumbersome? Regulation! Having spoken to regulators on this subject, they notice that there is an element in new offerings which does seem to be keeping them happy, rather than doing what's best for a client or end-user. The overriding message I received that day was *engagement with the end-user in the innovation process is paramount to success.*

It reminds me of a company I once worked for whose whole service process was based on protecting them from the client and the regulator. It was stark in its regard for the value, even purpose, that it offered the client. As you may guess it was not a programme I subscribed to for long.

So, perhaps it should come as no surprise that in February 2016 the Office of National Statistics announced that productivity in Britain's financial services sector has fallen significantly since 2009.

Measured by output per hour worked, the level of productivity in financial services was higher in the UK than in Germany, America, Italy and France between 2005 and 2009. This changed after 2009, demonstrating that the sector has been going in reverse with UK productivity now only slightly ahead of Germany and behind France, Italy and of course America. In my opinion this is a great shame, especially when London has always been such a major financial capital.

Innovation and disruption of existing models is, in my opinion, the only real way forward in making financial services and financial advice (along with many other heavily regulated businesses in the UK) accessible, stimulating and interesting to the general public. They are not engaged yet, and I predict that they will end up regretting this.

It's almost a *'would you buy it'* question. If you needed or were attracted to the market for the product or service area you are working on, and parking any natural bias to one side, can you see yourself taking up the new proposition you're offering? If yes, why? If no, why not — and what would you change?

Industry awards for innovation: are they worth it?

On the launch of our new innovative website, we entered a few competitions in order to test other expert views of our new offering. In the first year we were shortlisted for five awards over 2015 and were winners in three of them. We were delighted, especially with one award which was an outright win against some multinational companies. This was great for our business profile and of use to extend our reach on social media, as well as for press releases and features for the front page of the website. We think this was well worth the extra work as part of our ongoing development process. Even a shortlisting is a 'win' because it gets written about in the trade media.

We believe the most important part of entering the awards was also to raise our profile with possible 'suitors' whom we compete against at awards events. If you disrupt them enough, eventually they will come for you. Our website visitor analytics demonstrate the subsequent interest of big corporates in our innovations. We think this is well worthwhile in generating additional interest and the potential for a future business sale, without selling our main core business.

Despite the time commitment of submitting awards applications, any research in the approach you take, plus the cost of attending, we think this process is well worthwhile and a great way to raise profile within your industry and potentially even the national press.

If you are aiming for international recognition, then look for award programmes that meet your agenda and promote your proposition. I think it is fair to argue that awards are mainly an ego trip, rather than offering real value to the business or product. However, no one else is likely to put you forward, and adding 'Award Winning' to your marketing, social media and advertising campaigns is unlikely to be detrimental.

As I came towards the end of writing this book, I opened a fortune cookie with the message: "Somewhere, something incredible is waiting to be known." You have conviction that your new offering is incredible, it's just a question of: *is it known?* and possibly more importantly: *is it known by the right people?* If you want to raise the profile with the right companies, who could be suitors, find out what awards they won last year, find a category at the same event for this year, and make sure you are in the same room as them, with your new brand on the shortlists. They may not tell you immediately, but they will know about you far more quickly than letting nature take its course.

Scared of something different

Chapter Four: Construction

Construction: *the creation of an abstract entity*

It's been an awe-inspiring period of development time. Now, after much thought, challenging, personal disruption and pondering, it's time to stop.

It's time to start building!

You may plan to build the platform for your model yourself, or to outsource it, project managed by your team, or a mixture of both. If you are outsourcing, make sure there is clear documentation as to who owns the intellectual property before you start or share too much information on the overall plans and rollout.

However you plan to proceed, make sure that those working with you are capable. This may seem obvious, but you need to know that they share the same culture as you and have passion for their part of your dream right from the outset. Do they really share your vision of the future? Test it in whatever form you like, but if it's not there then don't engage. Without these shared qualities, your journey will be a lot harder and far less enjoyable.

Have you thought big enough? Even as a microbusiness, new technology and the delivery of innovation allow you to compete with even the biggest corporations. Does your new concept allow for volumes to work, and work well? Even if it was not originally your plan for a large competitor to buy it from you, have you allowed for a far greater capacity to be processed than you personally would want? If you have disrupted enough and the end users love it, will your invention simply collapse under the volume strain, leaving havoc in its wake? If you currently capture a zillionth of the market from your office, factory, studio or unit, and your new proposition, through internet and social media distribution, *could* predictably capture one per cent, and if you'd got it fabulously wrong and it was 10%, what would happen? Think this through and build accordingly.

Passion or profit

Business, for many people, is simply an issue of making money. There is some mileage in the sentiment that money makes the world go around. In my experience, however, it is *passion* that creates the most profit. If passion is your focus, then the money will normally follow. When we think about innovation, about disruption, to make things happen differently, then passion has to come before money. Of course, the end game may be your intention to streamline a process, improving profit and the money available from making the change. But it is not the money that is the motivator and it never should be. It's the personal passion, desire, even lust and energy to make change, to prove it can be done. *Without* this passion, the process of seeing the project through will be a whole lot harder. Passion can be extinguished very quickly, along with the end profits that could have been generated from the innovation.

More distribution, more profit, less work!
Direct to market

What is the priority for your business plans? Is quality a greater concern than profit? Is your brand alignment pitched in a way that dictates, to a greater or lesser extent, the level of profit that could ever be achieved? To some extent, as our main business has grown, we are starting to see the limits of the current model both in terms of production and also in terms of the profit that can be fairly achieved.

If you could *stack 'em high and sell 'em cheap* in your business, would you? You might be concerned about dilution of quality and would prefer not to take the risk, both in immediate sales and extra supply costs, and also in the longer term reputation of the brand. You may never have wanted to be seen as a discounter in your business and this suggestion may go utterly against the prestige value you have built up.

Our opportunity was to build another brand, deliberately unrelated to the first, with different values, ideals and opportunities designed to appeal to a younger demographic. I have written in previous books about the idea and value of effectively competing against yourself, as well of course as your competitors. There are many business examples of this, like the German prestige car manufacturers who have moved into small car production. Their main focus has been partly driven by emissions legislation across their brand range brought in by EU regulation; with this regulation change comes business change, opportunity and if achieved well, profit. This change has allowed manufacturers to compete and to capture far greater market share than before, also creating earlier loyalty to their brand.

However, could this concept change in direction apply to you and your plans, just not to your brand? The example above, of the motor manufacturers, is a good example of moving directly to a different market whilst maintaining local presence to create the possibility of national or even international exposure and client reach.

The main question has to be the speed at which competitors, and you, can access this identified target in a profitable way. This may mean deploying investment capital to access new markets through modern distribution channels. Are you ready — and is the market ready — for you to do this? Initially, don't get bogged down in thinking this through too far. There will always be times when your head tells you not to take action, while your intuition is to press ahead. My recommendation is always to go with your instinct; more often than not it is correct. Whether you think or feel 'no', others will do the same. On the other hand, if you are buzzing with a 'yes' then go with it.

The answer is not behind you — look ahead!

My Financial Services degree dissertation was on the subject of developing and delivering an online financial advice system in the UK. I completed that course and Honours degree in 2007. It is interesting to reflect on this document; what I perceived to be cutting-edge at the time has now been far surpassed by global innovation and technology especially in 'fintech'.

Enjoying a dose of nostalgia (because it might as well have been written a century ago), I was hoping to pick out some fascinating fact or concept from the past that was still relevant today. Not a bit of it: it was all virtually irrelevant to today's platforms. The pace of change has been phenomenal. I am proud to have been involved so early on, but I must never forget that I have to run if I want to keep up.

Finding renewed and enhanced future revenue value

Wealth shifts in waves across the nation and throughout the world. Like ocean tides, these wealth 'waves' are somewhat predictable, but the odd storm means that you can never be certain what's going to happen. Predicting future markets is similar and demographics can provide some guide to future outcomes. It was recently reported that those newly in retirement in the UK are now wealthier than those currently working under age forty-five. This was not the case in previous times.

However, with so many people living longer having enjoyed gold-plated pension accruals, to some extent this could have been predicted; this has to be seen against the backdrop of low pay rises for many years for those currently in work. Are demographics disrupting convention or creating opportunity? It's all change and it's what you do with the data that matters.

Squeezed margins

As an age category, those identified as 'Generation X' (usually defined as born between 1966 and 1980) are the 'squeezed middle' in financial terms. From a generational perspective, in my opinion, they are from a time that could be deemed a pre-tech bubble, with those currently aged under thirty (the 'Millennials') more likely to be the real wealth holders in future generations. This may have limited relevance to current business models now, although times are changing quickly, and this demographic observation is likely to have everything to do with business models in ten to fifteen years' time. If your business does not adapt and evolve to meet this change, are you effectively closing it ten years out?

A good example is the predictions, and significant opportunities, of the way future generations will do business within the personal finance sector, made by Deloittes Wealth Management in December 2015 in America. Projecting forward only a decade — and ten years is a long time in the financial services and technology worlds — Deloitte says 'robo-advisors' (automated financial advice systems/algorithm based systems) will capture 40% of the assets that millennials invest by the year 2025. These are powerful numbers when you consider the economy the estimates are based on.

Does this opportunity of change inspire you to be involved, or do you feel that this still leaves 60% for the traditional models? There will be a place for both. However, with automated advice usually being provided at low cost, and with face-to-face advice still expensive to deliver and market share swinging towards automation, the profitable days of traditional advice may have just had a 'sell-by' tag added to them.

Planning money

Having dreams and putting them into construction is a great progression. However, no project starts in earnest without money. It doesn't matter *what* you want to build; if there is no money to do it, you are going nowhere fast.

If you need financial backing, then seek it — but make sure you don't forego control just to get the funds. That would be a cause for huge regret in years to come when it is a great success.

As a personal example, we have had to give up income to afford the costs of development. I must admit to being less than entirely pleased about this, but if I want to be at the forefront of the breakthrough from our and the UK's traditional models, we needed to fund accordingly.

It is interesting to note that most traditional banks are not keen to lend to help these projects. They prefer to stick to their old lending modes for the protection of their own capital. Short sighted? Yes, especially with the growth in challenger banks, peer-to-peer lending and crowdfunding.

However you approach your plans, make sure you have access to funding all the way from development to launch, to ongoing servicing, to post-launch development and beyond. So many projects stall at vital stages, when confidence to move is required, only to be stifled by a lack of funding. Indeed, this is where many great innovative projects fail, possibly to the delight of the larger players who would prefer you not to disrupt their existing models or to integrate your great ideas into their new business launch. I would always recommend that you keep a budget reserve, at least 10%, for each year or each project component, holding over any unused reserve in addition to a new 10% reserve.

We have found that development costs do stretch by over 20% — but launch costs fall slightly. Be ready!

New business funding

Even this market has changed from the traditional High Street Bank model that ran in the past. With new 'challenger' banks coming to a High Street or internet site near you very soon, this is a great example of a cosy industry, controlled mainly by the 'big four' who some may argue have been complacent in their offerings to businesses across the UK. If this were not true, there would be no market for challenger banks, and no will from government to change regulation hurdles to allow others to enter the market.

It's a great example of 'you snooze; you lose'. Fintech has been one significant area of growth over the last few years. This is only now being embraced by the big banks, in terms of distribution and payment systems, whilst other companies are already way ahead of them. Touch-pay systems and even the Oyster Card are great examples of achieving small payments for the usual day-to-day services. The important point is that it is the user who is doing the work; technology reduces the need for human intervention, shrinking staff costs (among others) and getting funds to the provider more quickly.

Let's also not forget the new and aspiring alternatives, such as peer-to-peer lenders and 'business angels' who can offer alternative finance. At the time of writing, there is not much regulation of these, although I understand that the UK regulator has them in its sights, which will probably complicate things in the years to come. However, they are a great example of innovation in the application of a traditional model to a new market.

Crowdfunding has also come to the fore over the last few years. Unheard of five years ago, and really an anomaly in the finance world when it first started, it has gained traction and is now here to stay... unless the regulators deem that control is required. Somehow, I think they will.

Busy fool or busy focused?

You need to manage this transition (concept to construction) whilst keeping both hands on the tiller of your standard business. No one wants to be a busy fool! You probably work every hour you can physically spare anyway, and any new process you develop is going to extract all that fabulous data, experience and acumen that you have accrued over the years that got you to where you are today.

We have used a proportion of the profits from the main business to pay for the development of the new digital offering. You might call this self-funding. It has worked reasonably well, although it did create a few conundrums along the way when both business propositions got hungry for cash at the same time. This sort of thing keeps you on your toes, and is also a good challenge to your resolve. It could be suggested — in fact I *have* suggested — that the shelf life of our current model is probably only 15 years, as the 'Baby-Boomers' (people born between 1946 and 1964) go through the retirement process and into their twilight years.

The new online proposition, as far as we can see, has *no* shelf life, as long as it continues to be evolved and developed, challenging and disrupting previous ways of thinking on the way that (in our case) UK retail financial services are distributed.

Planning time

You are a business manager; therefore, you probably don't need me to tell you how to manage your time schedules. You must have worked out years ago what's best for you. However, as a business owner — large, medium or micro — you also know that adding a new project on the side will require thought and planning. You do not want to be a jack-of-all-trades and master of none. And rocking the business boat is going to challenge your schedule for both time and energy. Both of those things will require leadership if profits aren't going to suffer in the short or medium term.

You should consider adjusting development work time to allow for slower workload times in your normal main company production. Our own business has certainly experienced slower work months for some years during deep summer and deep winter; we choose to use that surplus time capacity productively by concentrating on our innovation plans at those points. This sort of timing can also help direct launch dates or updates to ensure that the main business workflow is not disrupted.

Put up or shut up!

From the initial plan — conceived on a wet Bank Holiday weekend after a put-up or shut-up conversation (in other words, argument!) — to research, to outsourcing, to costing, to checking, to market, to launch, took around nine months. This is a tall workload order in such a short timeframe and we were pleased with the official launch and a pre-launch appetiser for the media three weeks before that. The business team bought into the process very early on, admittedly after a sales pitch from me to explain the virtues, risks and, importantly, the extra work strain that all of us would have to bear. An innovation in disruption means swimming against the business tide anyway, so you need those who are going to be working on the project to join you at the outset.

We were also aware that the development and launch was only phase one. As an early adopter of conceptual change to the traditional model we were keen to be first to market, or very close to first.

Once launched, the service product was ready to use. In reality, we could have stopped there, but where would be the fun in that? In fact, the real work began at that point: the end of the build and launch. As part of a programme, we started to challenge each part of the process to improve, enhance and streamline what seemed to us were already leaps ahead of our expectations and those of our competitors. Additions have been made since then, and processes amended or reduced where possible to enhance the user experience.

Planning the 'after build/after launch' development is imperative to keep the disruption process going; this in itself will require business planning.

Time and money – your simple message

Writing a business plan for your new project is worthwhile, even vital, especially if you need your colleagues and associates to understand the real plan of action.

Just as important as the business plan is a marketing plan that is smart and clear. If you can't specify what you're trying to do, in one simple sentence, you're probably doing it wrong. This is because, in general, people's ability to absorb and retain something worthwhile has shortened dramatically over the past few years. The success of Twitter is a good example of this: if you can't say clearly what you mean in 140 characters or fewer, it's probably not worth saying. I think this is sad really, and that probably shows my age! However, I understand that for many people, even 140 characters will seem excessive; there are people who prefer even quicker message delivery, hence some preference for ideograms, such as Emojis.

The irony is that, at the time of writing this, current rumours are that Twitter is going to allow tweets to be longer than the current 140 characters. At one point, the news was reporting that it could be up to ten thousand words long. A real switch-off if ever there was one, subject to it coming true. I could serialise this entire book in around four or five tweets!

Of course, there are many forms of social media and communications, from Facebook to Instagram to Xing. I have my preferences and you will have yours, possibly all of the above, but your businesses involvement in these media is now mandatory to create interest around you, your business and your service or product.

Perhaps, with your plans complete, you could write a tweet that sums up your message. If you can't, then look at your real message again. From a business perspective, it's almost like the networking 'elevator pitch' we all learned we had to have back in the nineties: what you would say if you ever got into a lift with the one person you most want to influence and had just three floors to get them to 'buy' you, your plans or product, and need to know more, before the doors reopen and your target has gone.

A good contact I had, owned a party and entertainment business. His pitch was simple and brilliant when referring to his company: 'I sell fun!' It's clear, quick, concise, and most of all engaging. The line: 'I sell pensions' might have less effect — but 'I sell financial well-being' could pack more of a punch!

For this book, I might say: 'Challenge, disrupt, innovate, evolve your business. Do it because you can. Your core survival may depend on its future.' A quick core message of what this book covers and its challenge is to business owners and entrepreneurs who still have success as the core of their business desire. You may be able to think of alternative ways to express it — but the principle is established.

Clarity is key.

SME case study: KGW Family Law, Surrey

In the research for this book I had the pleasure of speaking to Karin Walker, of KGW Family Law. Karin is a collaborative divorce lawyer and mediator with whom I have worked closely in a professional capacity, and who has also undertaken a journey within her own professional service to create an online facility for public use.

In a similar way to our own arrangement, which is a separate online financial advice website, she has created an online facility which is a segmentation from her main website.

It was fascinating to confirm that she had certainly noticed that people wanted an online facility and that they preferred to look at their divorce situation post-mediation in their own time, without giving up any further time from their working day. Most of the financial settlements were completed through mediation, making the divorce process far simpler. Many of them were also keen to remove any potential for error by being able to organise the documentation online in their own time. She noted that this was of particular interest for those below the age of forty — the very people that we also have identified as a target market for online services.

In addition, she had realised that some other companies already had an online proposition which she felt was of lower quality (from lesser competitors offering average services for relatively high fees). To compete correctly, Karin wanted to offer a service from a professional organisation that provided good value in a correct manner and, to some extent, fended off lesser competitors. In her own words: *'A more bona fide and honourable approach than some of the others.'*

She noted that her business was a niche business, but had not taken long (around six months) to produce an online facility within her own services. With UK courts struggling to meet demand in divorce cases, the likelihood is that in future there will be a greater need for this type of online service. It also creates the opportunity for them to market other services that they may wish to offer, both now and into the future. I think this is an ideal platform.

Some of her less adventurous colleagues and competitors fear this new online proposition. However, Karin knows that that the fear of change is prevalent in us all. However, the future, particularly for the younger generations, is direct and online — irrespective of what professional services they require, from financial advice to getting divorced. Having a high quality, viable proposition in the market is vital. Also, being an earlier adopter of a good quality proposition is important for the future growth of the business. Your current business may have a potential 'shelf-life' of the length of the owners' work life, before they retire. An innovative and creative web offering extends the viable life of the business beyond this deadline, and also usually takes the focus away from the owner to a neutral position. This is highly valuable in making your business proposition more saleable in future times, especially where good revenue streams are evidenced.

It may take some time to get off the ground initially, and to keep going, and Karin was more than aware that the online offering may take some time to become profitable. But she also knows that it is a significant step for the future.

It is good that Karin shared some of the frustrations that she had encountered in preparing the new facility and the copious amounts of Terms and Conditions that need to be written both for the proposition and also for the website.

We enjoyed some mutual thoughts along the lines of *'seen it, been there, done that'for* the growing pains of achieving an online proposition, and she had experienced a delay of two months in being able to launch the facility. However, it demonstrates that resilience is a requirement to achieve and deliver the objectives.

Big Bang implementation

All industries and professions are innovating right now. It is the period to evolve. The financial services profession is no different. Indeed, during my 30 year involvement, I can only remember one similar time, back in the mid-1980s when equity markets moved to a deregulation of financial markets and also screen-based trading on computer platforms on the day dubbed 'Big Bang' in October 1986. Although systems have evolved significantly since this time, I believe it is only in the last few years that we have seen true innovation, rather than 'just' evolution.

There is much to discuss, too much for the context of this book. However, to provide a flavour of the change curve and dynamic and disruptive thinking that crosses every aspect of our business, the following World Economic Forum diagram is a reasonable way of looking at the current position.

The following diagram is reproduced with kind permission from the World Economic Forum Project, Final Report, June 2015 entitled 'The Future of Financial Services: How disruptive innovations are reshaping the way financial services are structured, provisioned and consumed'.

The first consolidated taxonomy for disruptive innovation in financial services

The future is awesome, the past is history….but a good place to know where you started.

43 and below/'The Tech Wing'

In 1985, I left sixth form school with a couple of A levels and a rather apathetic, laissez-faire attitude to education. I joined a bank at the end of that year and became involved in thirty years of UK retail financial services. It's been a great journey and there's more to come. In the last year of this school education, I was asked to do another GCSE (or 'O Level' as it was still called then) to fill in my curriculum.

I chose Computer Studies, which was new to everyone. Two large black boxes were installed in a small tutorial room and this became 'the tech wing' — a first for a Surrey school, both in terms of having a room or indeed computers! It's still mind-boggling to consider that something we take today as the norm is in fact only been a staple of our lives for around twenty-five to thirty years. I still laugh at the amended 'Maslow's hierarchy of needs' diagram with Wi-Fi now appearing at the very bottom as a basic human need.

Indeed, having recently caught up with a friend whom I went to school with, and who was crammed into the same 'tech wing' as I was, we also suggested that had we known 30 years ago that we would have sat in front of a computer for most of our lives, first we would not have believed it, second we would not have wanted it, and finally that we might have paid more attention. I don't think either of us passed the O Level, by the way!

This raises two important points for me. One is that the 'sitting in front of a computer' may end soon. With 5G mobile compatibility on its way, and the mobile 'ecosystem' about to explode, will we need offices and desks at all? Flexible working in the use of both time and place will reach new heights. My favourite place to write is on a plane and in fact I am tapping out this particular page of text at 39,000 feet. The other point is that people below about the age of about forty-three have never known a world without computers. Everyone over this age has had to *adapt* to accommodate this new tech opportunity, as it has become available to the masses and to businesses.

This threshold may not be scientific but is a good parameter to demonstrate the thinking of people above and below this age, and to question yourself as a business owner to see which group you naturally engage with. Preferably you should engage with both — but as we have found, you may need to create diverse business models to achieve this utopia in the real world.

All areas of business are innovating right now; changing processes, perceptions and ideas about how something can be arranged in a better way. Failing to move with technology changes can hinder your progress when you do want to move forward.

I understand that the NASA Space Shuttle programme stopped, not because it was not a success, but because the electronic systems had not been updated as the programme, and technology, moved forward — effectively bringing the project to an end.

I am sure you can create a similar diagram to that illustrated earlier, for your own profession, focusing on one or two specific areas of expertise and knowledge. The intellectual property you have collated and are using is unique to your business now, and to the proposition you are working on. You would only share part of this once released in full to the market, and we are the same. We hope to share with you our passion to innovate, even disrupt, to prove that a concept can work and to deliver it to market in a competitive end user-focused offering. The failures, the challenges, the niggles, and the successes of our journey led to the launch in January 2015 of SaidSo.co.uk, our online financial advice site.

I am no tech expert, believe me, but others around me are pretty cool with it. You too can outsource to others the job of embracing 'younger' and more dynamic thinking than your own, so that it can be applied to your existing traditional business.

All I needed was a phone! Historic communication change

Twelve or so years ago I got divorced. I had been divorced before and, eventually, the financial settlement was agreed and sealed.

Not having much money left after that, my preference was just to have a telephone. As long as I could get in contact with my peers, colleagues and contacts, I should be able to survive. And this proved to be the case. How times have changed since then for me, and my contacts in terms of both communication and telephony.

Communication methods are now very different and far more interesting. There are those who would suggest they are also more intrusive. This might be a poor state of affairs for the individual and a great one for creating business opportunities. The use of the telephone to communicate is in decline and seems to have become outdated, even unacceptable to many younger people. With preferences moving towards email and social media in its many forms, using tablets, mobile technology and the like — all of which can still be intrusive — these options are potentially less immediate if you want to maintain control.

Far greater information and visuals can be imparted, faster than ever before. And when we remember that the internet and its possibilities are only in their infancy, it's clear that this trend will only continue. The latest widespread use of GIFs is a case in point, allowing significant quantities of information to be provided in a short burst of data.

This physical communication change offers an opportunity to reach far greater audiences than before, and should be factored into your planning for the reach of your project. Telephone selling is largely no longer acceptable; end users expect to select how to communicate with you. They can now access a lot more information and the power of choice is vital. You've just got to make sure you are in the market and visible to the people you want to attract, communicate with and sell to.

Is the original end game still the end game, or did reality bite you on the backside?

When I founded our main business, my main short term focus was to get it started and running. Thinking you can run a business, starting it and then getting it to profitability are three very different things, as you will know. Developing it further is the next objective, either in physical size (staff, customer base, premises) or business volume, possibly keeping the enterprise small, maintaining quality volume, and hopefully high profitability.

Your objective may be a bit of both; we all have different plans... but be clear what yours are.

Scared of something different

Chapter Five: Incubation

Incubation: *unique and highly flexible combination of business development processes, infrastructure and people designed to nurture new thinking*

I used a different dictionary to define incubation, and therefore it could be fairly argued that this definition itself is innovative. However, it works well in summarising the process of incubation and creativity, and embodies our thinking in the culture of our own journey.

With your basic business construction complete, and the evolution stage moving from innovation to production, you need to stand by your brand and product. I was asked about this recently at a fintech forum. To be frank, I was surprised by the question: if you do not wholeheartedly believe in your own mission, it's unlikely that anyone else is going to get animated about it. Belief is contagious and needs to be spread from the head of the project to everyone else including the end user.

There is something satisfying about this element of a project. It's like writing a book: the body is created, the chapters have been formed, the title is ready, and the end message is nailed. However, there is still so much to write! You still have to draw together all the threads you have created into one bound document that you will be proud to put your name and brand on. You need to feel sure you'll still smile every time you see it on a virtual bookstand, knowing that there is part of you within those pages.

Incubator of things

For many of us, just doing the day job is enough to fill the diary — sometimes with work spilling over into our spare time. To some extent, I thrive on managing all that needs to be achieved, although I am not certain what the real price of this will be. Time will tell. If we stopped at this very point, just doing what we do now, our mould would never be broken, but would not progress.

To help avoid getting stuck in this phase, I like to have an 'incubator of things'. This is a marked place to park all those innovations, plans, disruptive thoughts and ideas, to keep them together. For me, it's an electronic file and a pile of paper on my desk that everything goes into. It doesn't pollute the main work until we are ready to make significant changes. It allows me, and importantly others, to go into the data at any time, to add, to challenge or just to understand what's being considered. You do want others to do just this; to look, to share, to challenge, even to annoy them. If they share your vision and culture of the possible, the reality will be even better. It is usually sensible to build in a timeline to keep progress in line with your launch plans. You do not want to be late to market with innovation, allowing competitors to steal a march on you. There are few silver medals in business.

Correspondingly, those who instinctively prefer the even keel of no change, "it works, so don't fix it!" should be firmly guided away during the build stage. They have their own great value in their outlook, in allowing you the time to lead this innovation, and will be valuable later on in testing the end product or service. The views of these 'safe pairs of hands' do matter at the *right* time, but you cannot afford to let them zap your brainwave juices before you even try them out. They may well slow the progress of the build process, as we noted in Chapter One.

There is only a little structure to the incubator. Segmenting it along the lines of the current practice will probably succeed only in creating a model similar to the one you already have. Indeed, *reversing* the structure might be more productive. You might even find that the current system you're using could be improved upon with the new process. We certainly found this with a few aspects of our existing planning process. The new offering is interactive and engaging, whilst the older incarnations seem flat by comparison, although it is informative and can easily be improved upon.

We chose to launch the whole innovation in one go, with a short pre-launch campaign to whet consumer and media appetites. We have then added updates each quarter since, as our preference is to be an early adopter of change. You may prefer to introduce your new approach over an agreed period, especially if the new thinking is very radical, and I hope it is.

Whatever you do, create a separate space for your planning and incubation, both in reality and in your mind. Clear, unpolluted thinking is required to make any significant difference. Remember, your *incubator of things* is packed with high value intellectual property, so keep it secure and only viewable by those whom you trust. Imitation may be the highest form of flattery — but this sentiment doesn't apply to a new business idea. This is why we have a whole legal industry based around intellectual property, to provide you with a mechanism to protect your innovative ideas.

The power of attention to detail

Ideas! Creativity! Wow, they are both so exciting. From appearing in your mind, to becoming a detail in a sketch or working document, to wanting it finished and out in your target market, can take seconds. The energy-filled rush is, and should be, fantastic. The reality is usually *not*.

In my opinion, when you are transferring conceptual thinking to innovation, and ultimately to production, attention to detail is everything. And although you can and should have deadlines, do not hold firm to them if the quality of your innovation is going to be compromised by poor quality output caused by a lack of attention to detail. You want to *wow!* the market — and if you can't get past those minor errors in production your output is likely to be dismissed.

My mother has observed that I can be obsessive. This is probably the reason why I have been divorced a couple of times. But the notion can also be seen as a compliment. For our business to be able to deliver our online proposition to a quality that competes on even terms with the big banks, insurance companies and new well-funded corporate entrants, we needed the attribute of a stickler for detail to get the launched product ready for scrutiny by our end-users and the prying minds of our competitors. The analytics on visitor paths for website traffic that you can interrogate from Google statistics make very interesting reading; you can see exactly which pages institutions are visiting and what they are concentrating on.

This process of detail — checking, even triple-checking — cannot be rushed. Never fool yourself with the belief that it can. From idea to launch took us 'just' nine months, and that was with the benefit of good experience behind us before we started. This counts as a rapid turnaround. Whatever you do, ensure that the quality of that final delivery is not sped through at the cost of quality. This is a false economy; it is better to be late to market but correct, than early and wrong.

Strength of brand

Your innovation is produced, all shiny and new, and in your eyes and those of your colleagues it's awesome. You have moved through concept, to innovation, to production. From its release it needs to be incubated, nurturing the new thinking. Now, what are you going to call it? You can't just call it a widget! The strength of your concept and creation has to be represented just as strongly through your new name and brand as the concept itself.

Just like your innovation, no one can have used the new brand name before. The new name, along with its visual image, has to be available for you to use. You must check every register and trade mark registration, Companies House, your industry's regulator and the like.

We developed the image of our brand, having secured the brand name and, of course, trademarked it. To trade mark both the name and the visual image of the brand, namely two applications, is both sensible and relatively inexpensive. Having achieved this, our outsourced (and younger) colleagues created a cleaner, more dynamic, variation on our theme which we preferred, so we needed to go back to the trademark office to get this image lodged accordingly. Our brand logo is now 'of its time' and I am sure it will need a revisit to modernise it in another few years or so, as many brands do.

Securing a trademark does not mean that you are fully protected from competitors. Indeed, your application may even attract the attention of challengers before you really want it to. However, it gives you far greater legal protection than *not* having it. Take good legal advice and follow it.

The new name has to reflect the passion and vision you have put into the new creation — but also its value position as you move into the future. Focus on the demographic you want to attract, take guidance from that audience, testing ideas with them as you go. You want them to 'buy it', so ask them for their views, however positive or critical they are.

Think about any selected brand, both now and also in five and ten years' time. Will the new name still seem un-dated, despite the passage of time? Most importantly, I know that *you* would buy your new product, it's your baby after all — but would you buy the *brand*? Which would you buy first: brand or product? If there is a straight answer to this, you need to revisit the new brand and improve it. Why?

You want the *brand name* to be what users apply to the product, rather than the product itself — in the same way that 'Hoover' became a generic term for any vacuum cleaner. However you finally focus on your brand, take pride in it, for it contains a bit of you within it. You have supported its birth, production and growth this far, so you need to keep going with it.

The new product launch is only the beginning

It does not take an actual rocket scientist to tell you that it takes an army of people much time to get a space rocket to a launch pad. And once the burners are going and launch has been achieved, that is not the end of the mission. It is the beginning.

This is *not* rocket science. However, the same principles apply to your product/service/concept launch. I found myself almost spellbound by our product. Its development took it to a far higher stratosphere (excuse the pun) than I could have ever imagined. But remember: a business approach is required at all times, from costs, to promotion, to management, to social media and onwards. Just because you've got a great idea and have been able to develop it, so what? It happens every day, with many businesses failing to make a success of it, and your concept may be no exception. The inventor of the vacuum cleaner, Hubert Cecil Booth (1901) was a successful man, but it was Hoover that became known for the household product. Strength of brand? Probably.

Once the exhilaration of development is complete and your launch has been a success, remember to plan the business model for the first few years. It is likely to be in those early days that it will attract interest and approaches from those who want to acquire your model, or endeavour to plagiarise it. This 'compliment' will gain you no friends, but you need to be aware that it's likely to happen. Just ensure you stay ahead of the change curve.

The market *we* are focusing on, which is the online distribution of UK retail financial advice, is only in its infancy. So, we believe that some competition is an advantage in raising the profile of the opportunity to the public. We envisage eventually around ten to fifteen serious contenders in the online financial advice market before some consolidation occurs. It needs a plan; both a business plan, and planning for any additional developments that you'll aim to add as you evolve and incubate the platform further.

For example, for our online financial advice system, SaidSo.co.uk, we offered additional free guides and a special offer at our first anniversary. This involved an effective 'facelift' of the front pages to engage further with the UK public. We had also looked at subtle changes after around nine months, but deferred these to the anniversary to give a greater emphasis on the updated offering. We also made a business decision not to make any changes at all for at least three months after that. The thinking behind this plan is that further evolution in such quick succession could be disruptive to the very disruption that we had already applied, creating the potential for confusion. I hope that's not confusing!

Change is good. Change for the sake of change is not.

We have certainly felt pressure, real or perceived, even from our own web developers who are in our target age range, to reduce the consumer price point. As we approached our first anniversary, as a promotion, we introduced a limited time discount (£100 off in 100 days, about a one-third reduction in initial pricing) with the aim of extending usage, engaging interest further and further adding to our research on the concept price point of this innovation. This has now ended and proved to be a great way to gather even more fresh data on the end user experience.

Promotion

We also want to analyse the outcomes of the free guides and lower price offering. Therefore, after 100 days we will return the price of our advice service to its original level and assess the outcomes over the summer. The promotion has been clearly positive, and on review we may permanently reduce the price to the lower level to create volume. This is only a minor price manipulation compared to what some of our competitors can achieve, and we will look at this position further once the data and its tracking starts to become clear.

We are certainly breaking new ground, for ourselves and partly for our profession, so we know there is no single right answer. You have to start somewhere and then adjust, otherwise we could find ourselves bogged down in unnecessary procrastination... which is the arch enemy of both creativity and delivery.

The entrepreneur Elon Musk is credited with saying: "Failure is an option here. If things are not failing, you are not innovating enough." If our promotion is not successful, we will reconsider the programme. We certainly do not want to race to the bottom on price.

Race to the bottom

Consumers are normally price-sensitive, especially with regard to a new product line or innovation that does not have a current comparable. So, they may compare the new creation to the one that it renders obsolete; in which case, what should the new price be? There is a discussion to be had in working out what the market will tolerate. Surveys and consumer testing may help here, although the previous alternative (in whatever format that was) may still guide price and with it initial margins.

Any misguided manager can skip profit and race to the bottom on their price point to win business. This is not a wise move for the future prosperity of a new opportunity. The downward journey on price is easy, especially for large corporations. Slashing initial profit to increase initial distribution and market share is nothing new, and may be a simple solution to a product launch, especially if the product is price sensitive, as many mainstream items are. You will see this every day with introductory offers, and we have partially embraced this tactic with our first anniversary promotional discount. However, the journey back on price increases is a wholly different matter, and it has the potential for your business to shoot itself in the foot in the longer term.

Having written this initial thinking, we now find ourselves in the position where a major High Street bank is offering their version of an advice facility — at the same price as ours.

So, manage your price tactics carefully. Always bear in mind long term profitability and product sustainability.

News follows price

It has been suggested recently that news follows price, rather than the other way round. When trends in investing move negatively, the press output follows the market and vice-versa. It is not the press reporting that sets the market. Some may perceive this to be a reverse psychology, but it is not. If sentiment, which is usually driven by price, is against an investment, the price will fall. The reverse is also true.

Does this extend to product? And its innovation?

Why the end price?

In life, as you already know, things are not always what they first appear. The reason why something happens, or doesn't happen, or annoys you, may not be for the reason you think. For example, an international airline may charge what appear to be high increments for any ancillary benefits you may choose, but on top of a low basic purchase price. Why?

For certain there is a marketing benefit to this low price point situation and there are companies that rightly promote this with gusto. However, the air fares themselves are subject to tax, whereas the ancillaries may not be. So there may be a benefit to the company in attracting new passengers — and also to the more seasoned consumer, if they can bear to give up a few ancillaries. Therefore, what might irritate some people could actually become a benefit. Turn the proposition the other way around, so that the initial cost is higher, but with no or limited ancillary costs, the overall cost would work out higher; in this case the consumer would probably look around for a cheaper flight and of course remain annoyed about the subsequent ancillary costs.

Examples of ancillaries (reasonably expected as standard by the passenger but charged by the airline) might be using the toilets on one budget airline for €1 per visit. However, the initiative saves the airline time and maintenance cost, plus disposal costs, and emptying costs which are usually taxed. Twenty minutes to landing and there's always a huge queue for the toilets… but when people have to pay, there is no queue! So the budget airline can remain a budget airline, allowing them also to keep their turnaround times shorter, allowing more flights out of the same plane. The base transport model has not been disrupted, but the way it is planned is innovative and profitable.

There is a mass of tax legislation around the globe that in part dictates the cost of a product. You only need to fill your vehicle up with fuel to know this. When you stand at the pump, you will know what choices you have to make between petrol, diesel, gas. Each has a different tax bracket and each provides a different solution to the same issue of getting you from A to B. All are designed to be better than the first, and will probably all be usurped by electric cars in the future. They are all based on the same idea, just a different application, and of course electric cars will be taxed more highly when a sufficient volume has been reached. I suppose the one thing that will never change is that the Chancellor will always need the tax revenue; he or she will just have to change (innovate) to ensure it keeps rolling in!

Taking this further, if your new offering is radical, and I hope it is, will it be taxed in a different class to current models, with different tax rates applying? You might want to check this, just in case.

There are offers that look to be 'too good to be true'. To be honest, they usually are. 'Caveat emptor' (buyer beware) is always great advice. However, when you're thinking around how any offer, promotion or deal got to where it is, your time would be well invested seeking to understand the methodology of how those making the offer got to where they did. Was it profit, was it market share, was it a bean counter's diktat, was it perceived exclusivity, was it just what the existing market would tolerate? The reality is that it is probably a mixture of all the above — but the last point is key, namely *what the existing market will tolerate*.

We are looking at disrupting the existing market with innovation. What will this new thinking and approach do to the price that the end user pays? You can push product price up because the end user sees a real 'value-add' to his or her experience. You can change perceptions so people will pay the same price for a lesser model. Some car manufacturers seem to have achieved this in recent years, charging the old high price for smaller, and some might argue, lesser models, whilst pushing up the price of the larger models to create higher revenues overall. Or will the "stack 'em high" approach be more applicable, selling more units for less money, relying on volume to achieve your monetary objectives? This approach can work, although many experts today argue that this is the harder route to success and requires sufficient infrastructure to cope with volumes.

Price in many situations is a sensitive touch-point for purchasers. This is not always the case, but often. When preparing your new innovation, this is one time when I would *not* start with the end in mind. Price in itself could well disrupt and confuse the real differences you want to make. However, once you have established the parameters of your concept, have a look at what it might achieve; the cost to build, market and deliver (you will do this anyway for sure, but add a margin) in terms of both money and time. And then check what the end price might be. Let's face it, it's got to be worth your energy; if not, what can you change to make it so?

When we considered our new online-only approach to financial planning, we started by dissecting the costs in terms of time and money. Starting with time, we wanted the end consumer to be able to control when and where they chose to do their planning. Consumer control is paramount to the end user which has been propelled further by mobile connectivity, and this trend will continue. Most people want to be (or at least to feel) in control of their decisions and actions. We wanted to streamline the process, to make it logical and as far as possible user friendly (not always that easy in financial services with its lengthy compliance 'red tape'). We believe that we have largely achieved this and wanted our brand to reflect this open approach.

Having figured this out, next we looked at the process we currently used and its cost compared to delivering financial advice online. The face-to-face model has to take into account meetings, post, telephone calls and costly human interaction which can be largely stripped out of the model. There are systems available that take this to an extreme in automating the entire process, including the advice; we stopped short of this because we believe that the end product should have a real adviser providing real advice, although the *middle* section can be largely automated. It is the time cost that adds to the overall cost that is vital here. Stripping out the meetings and their ancillary parts saves over half the time spent on the process, which in turn reduces our costs by half before we start. This saving is obviously significant and can be used in the pricing of the end product.

New infrastructure costs are usually high at the start of building a system to deliver a new service. We have already noted in this book the financial and business support that many countries provide to start-ups and innovation. In the UK, you may be able to offset tax with a Research and Development claim — and you may want to check this with your tax advisors at the outset. If it can be done, this may mean that the overall costs are lower, or that you may be able to push your budget out further for more development because of any tax allowance.

Volumes

With our new direct to client (D2C) online business now fully developed, our existing infrastructure could struggle to cope with the volumes of business that could be created, however profitable the model is. This statement is made with the presumption of reasonable market penetration.

Although we were aware of this potential problem, our business has the ability to create some additional capacity to cope with additional volume, certainly in the shorter term, although it may require 'all hands to the pump' at all times. The team have bought into this possibility and are positive about their ability to cope. The management time taken to create the new business line is a case in point, which it could be argued is now surplus time as an example. The infrastructure could and will handle the initial uplift and then we will carry out a review.

One final alternative, if we prove *too* successful, is simply to take the new website down for an agreed time.

That's a rather Armageddon approach to a potential problem, definitely the one of last resort, but it is always an option.

This brings our management to an important junction when thinking about the potential ways forward for infrastructure development and additional ideas innovation. We could expand to cope initially, without increasing our advertising spend. However, our main focus as an objective is the proof of concept — and then, rather than operate it ourselves in the longer term, to sell it along with the data, activity flow models, charts and income stream created. We hope that the combination of our marketing, social media, award wins and disruption of standard models will attract the right attention. Our analytics suggest that interest from the right type of suitors is high and we hope to build this even further.

The key point of our new concept, as it should be for any new innovative product created, is 'does it have a sustainable income model at the end?' If not, we'd have to think again.

If the sale option fails, our fall-back position is to build the new business line SaidSo.co.uk further, investing further into our infrastructure, as volumes build.

Would you sell it?

Assuming you achieve the objective of disrupting your own business market, you are inevitably going to upset people in the current business area along the way. That's good news! However, be under no illusion that you are also going to attract suitors who like the difficult work you have put in and want to take the model off your hands...

or close it down if they see it as too much of a threat in their own development. We have seen many examples of this. Competitors constantly need to adapt, grow, and find new ways of increasing their own market share and distribution. If they can buy it off your shelf, all the better, although some might prefer to copy and replicate your ideas. The importance of taking good advice and securing your intellectual property is therefore paramount.

In the mid to late 1980s, insurance companies bought up estate agent chains to sell their mortgage-related products on the back of the house sales. A tenuous D2C type model of buying distribution, the model applied by many of the large UK life insurers relied on volumes which worked for a while, until the economic recession of 1991 which saw most business models fail. Many estate agents bought their own businesses back at a fraction of what they had sold them for a few years earlier.

But do be ready to sell! The risk is that your new proposition is *so* good that it will render your traditional model defunct and irrelevant. If you sell if for enough cash, then you can run the old business off, picking and choosing the work that remains profitable and enjoyable.

Think about the real value of the new business model you are creating, both now in its infancy and later when it starts to reach some maturity. Also look at its real value when up to full capacity, with the correct marketing and advertising behind it. Many vibrant fledging enterprises are snapped up in their infancy and you will need to be confident, with a real value price in your mind, if you are approached early.

Surprises do happen!

Scared of something different

Chapter Six: Revolution

Revolution: *a forcible overthrow of a government or social order, in favour of a new system*

What about the forcible overthrow of a concept that has been in use for years? Business revolution is awesome to be a part of. There is a partisan spirit that flows through the office, with troops fighting secretly against occupying forces, namely tradition and the status quo.

We have both a traditional model and a disruptor living side by side, and I thank my team for not mixing them up. Their capacity has been firmly tested and not found wanting. It's a bit like the original Ghostbusters film: *"Don't cross the streams..."* YET!

I love the thought of revolution. I have a saying: 'If I could start again, I would not start from here!' Think about it: if you could take those existing methods, systems, administration and just ditch the lot and start again, where would *you* start? Of course, you'd keep some components — but I would like to hypothetically wager you have a list of five things in your head right now that would change right away. So, why don't you?

The power of revolution needs to be handled with care. It can be used positively for change, but it can also turn against you if you do not take the key components of your project, your people, with you. We have seen casualties along the way, where confusion has led to frustration leading to the inevitable exit. Observe, identify and help where you can to keep everyone motivated and engaged.

Revolution of the people, by the people

Disruption is nothing new. The French Revolution of 1789-1799 must have been an awe-inspiring time... as long as you survived. Inspired by radical and liberal ideas, it was a brutal time of uprising of the people, for the people. The guillotine was kept busy dealing with those who did not toe the party line — and from a modern human resources or political correctness perspective, that is an unacceptable way to motivate your team to stick with you.

Modern times have seen less bloodthirsty examples of the power of the people, exemplified by Solidarność (Solidarity), first emerging as a Trade Union not controlled by the Communist government that was in power in 1980. It took nearly a decade for Solidarity to finally reach power, in a democratic fashion, in late 1989.

However, it was the people themselves, their social movement, who were motivated to make significant change. So much so that they influenced human history forever. Those were inspirational times, with people seeking a better future, and that is what innovation is all about. But *without* the people on your side the chances of real change are slim and the chances of survival even slimmer!

In this chapter we have looked at some of the additional challenges that you may face, should your intentional disruption turn into the nightmare of a staff revolution.

The staff are revolting

You can interpret the title of this section in any way that suits your own views — and yes, my own team *has* read this!

As an SME business owner it is easy to forget that your staff are your biggest asset. However, the conundrum is that the wrong team can also be your biggest liability. The issue for many business owner/managers is that the switch from positive to negative can be quick and, as we have experienced, unprovoked, unexpected and disappointing.

It is probably unreasonable to expect a staff member ever to be as enthusiastic, conscientious or hard-working as you are yourself. This is one of the reasons many companies offer equity incentives to staff to give them that owner/ manager experience of sharing profits. If you are fortunate enough to find an employee who is as committed as you are, do whatever you can to retain them because they are like gold dust!

We know that money is not always a motivator; many philosophies and popular theories will confirm this point. But if you upset your staff, can you recover your position should you want to keep them? Trains of thought can change quickly, with income suddenly becoming a motivator. How many times have you said to yourself: *"I'm not paid enough to take/do/sell/administer this"*? More importantly, if you have said it within your *own* business, your staff may be thinking along similar lines.

That does not mean that an individual cannot be expendable, no matter what they do. You will have heard the saying that you are only as good as your last deal. But having a trusted, focused team player makes life much easier for a business owner.

When we were away on our annual leave one year, we had a young employee who stayed late, very late, in the office one cold December evening, to check that the office was secure after a fire in the adjacent building. This employee only stayed with us for a year as it was her first job after leaving school, whilst she was thinking further about what track she really wanted to follow. Emailing from afar, we were grateful to have her focus where others might have begrudged the chore or avoided it altogether. The young employee concerned treated our company as her own when we were not there, but there was a reason for her dedication: she was a family member. But most of all, she *cared.*

Family members can make good employees or terrible employees. They are often very loyal, dependable and trustworthy. But there is always a flip side to each situation, and they can also be lazy. You also have to remember that, if a family member does something wrong, the same employment rules apply to them as would apply to any other member of staff. If you ever have to use your company's disciplinary procedures, which may not make for a pleasant next family gathering depending on how close a family member they are, then be comfortable in yourself that you could apply such rulings. The option not to discipline a family member correctly sends the wrong message of family favouritism to your other staff, which can then lead to resentment and understandable discord in the rest of the team.

This leads on to the whole subject of your employees, and making the most of them — keeping the good ones and losing those that don't quite cut the mustard. This can often be the case with some sales people, whose best ever sale was to the business owner in the first place, after which they consistently failed to meet their agreed and no doubt challenging targets or project objectives.

Motivation

As an employer and innovator you will also have to think about the way you can motivate and retain your staff.

As I write this, I do question what companies' policies, targets and profit-driven ethics are doing to their staff in the long term. I know people in their late forties and early fifties who are already thinking about, or actively engaging in, leaving work permanently.

As an employer, ask yourself: *'What makes my employees want to come to work on a Monday morning and not put their CV on a job site the night before, rather than the thought of propping up their tedious work space?'*

The process of recruiting good staff is not easy. There are too few well-qualified, confident people looking for work. Those who are good know they can command a high salary with benefits, and are usually snapped up before they ever 'make it to market', having been spotted (or poached) by some shrewd manager/owner along the way. What are you doing to stop your employees from changing job?

Retention

Staff retention is important for innovation and disruption. You need the confidence of stability, and loyalty within your individual staff members and as a team, to provide the platform to create and disrupt. Without it, we believe, the distraction of keeping the team cohesive will reduce the impact of the end delivery.

How can you control the situation and incentivise staff to make them want to stay? Many of the ideas, philosophies and processes start with a simple truth: placing trust in your staff. If you distrust your employees, they will sooner rather than later lose motivation and that is the very reason why you are thinking about these issues!

As an employer, you will probably know that your employees can ask for any of the following points to be applied to their contract. Some authorities suggest these are 'hygiene factors'. Irrespective of this view, they might be vital to the long term viability of an important team member:

> ***Flexible working*** — Many companies, large and small, use this facility now, usually based around a 'core hours' structure, where there is a proportion of the day when everyone is in. The option invariably relies on trust from both parties. You trust that your employee is in at the times they say they are. So, if you come in at 9am, and someone says they were in at 6am, you have to believe that they were. It relies on the business manager or owner to know if this really happened. It won't take long to work this out if it is not the case.

> Flexible working can work very well, especially if you have some employees who are at their best first thing in the morning, or others that work well in the evening. Play to their natural strengths. If

you are asking for big energy to be applied to an important project, you cannot expect this from 9.01 every morning to 7.05 each night. Some employees really enjoy working in the office alone with no disruptions, no email and no telephone or background noise. Others enjoy the buzz of camaraderie, and will be at their best at different times of the day. If you observe, each has its value that needs to be nurtured within a project. You do not want a bunch of clones when innovating; you want people to break out, to be free thinkers, to challenge, but to combine at the end and be proud of their part in the process.

Compressed working — A slightly newer working practice in the UK, it is sometimes worth considering a compressed hours system for some. Effectively, it means allowing individuals to work the hours they want (say thirty-five hours a week) at the times that suit them. So if they want to work Monday to Thursday lunchtime in large time blocks, then take Thursday afternoon and Friday off, they can because they have completed their allotted hours.

I have experienced a nine-day working fortnight, in the form of 70 hours for the usual two-week period (ie ten working days) compressed into nine days. Personally, I am not a fan of this system and I feel its success may depend on the type of profession or industry you operate in.

There also has to be an understanding between employer and employee. It might start to unravel if employees build in time for visiting doctors and dentists in *your* time, but are then using their free time effectively at your expense.

I once worked for a company where many of the employees had institutionalised overtime. They worked at least an extra hour every day, which was all billable to the client. Once compressed hours working was introduced, a different process of engagement occurred. The billable hours went down; the employees left the office an hour earlier each day, and still produced the same amount of work. Although I was only an observer, it appears they had slowed their work rate in order to be able to charge for the overtime. Under the new system, their focus became time-driven.

This is only one example that had the unforeseen consequence of reducing income to the business, while potentially not improving staff costs. Correspondingly, if staff costs can be reduced and billing left the same, then there is potential for improved profitability.

If you feel that compressed hours are not for your company, but your employee requests this, you can refuse, but there are set grounds on which this can be done. ACAS, the conciliation service, has a very useful document on this and this is noted in the reference section.

Job sharing — Two (or more) people do the same job, sharing time, and of course, salary. I don't think I need to explain this one.

Staggered hours — The employees have different start, finish and break times from other workers, giving a spread of cover at all times, with the potential to reduce overall costs. This option is close to the flexible working process, but planned to advantage the company. This could be extended to a work-shift process.

Home working — As an employer we have to trust our staff that if they are working from home, they are *working* from home. The success or otherwise of this option may depend on your location and the infrastructure (particularly broadband) position of the employee's home. Judging by our own home, which is five miles from a major UK town, but may as well be another galaxy (apologies to any Martians reading this), this proposition would be pointless.

Home working... the real future?

Many experts predicted that, a decade ago, home working and its derivatives were the future, with many major corporates citing their plans for this type of flexibility over the years. However, the reality we have experienced seems not to have occurred in the volumes anticipated. This failure could in part be levelled at the UK infrastructure systems that have failed to roll out suitably fast broadband and fibre-optic services across the UK. Also, the availability of suitable commercial property and office space has meant that the need for volume 'hot-desking' in the fight for space has not occurred in the volumes first anticipated.

This situation seems to be static, even when taking into account the recent law change in allowing commercial property to be switched to residential high-end luxury homes. Centre Point in London is an excellent (and large) example, with sales going fast at the time of launch. Promises are in the pipeline for ungraded 'super-fast' broadband throughout the country, and this may allow home working really to take off; although at the time of writing, promised parameters are being curtailed, particularly in rural areas. Systems development has and will of course continue to grow to enhance this opportunity.

You can introduce a psychometric test system to see whether your employees are suitably independent and focused to work from home or whether they will 'swing the lead'. However, many companies are looking at online initiatives so the team can work from home, which can be anywhere in the world!

If you feel that you cannot entertain, or your business or project will not afford, changing the working hours or other conditions that you need to deploy for a work contract, there may be other options open to you. Examples that could be considered to offer your staff to aid retention include: —

> ***Share save style schemes*** — As with any small to medium enterprise, sometimes known as an SME, this remuneration option is probably something you may want to avoid, or at least to tread carefully with. This is not advice, but it's your company, your equity and you have worked hard for your money. You probably want to keep it rather than give it away! This is a not unreasonable sentiment; however, if your staff feel they own a bit of the business, however small, they are likely to show

greater loyalty and this is evidenced by many thriving and dynamic US corporations. Team members will often work harder because if they improve the profits and ultimately the company, they will gain greater value. There are many examples of similar types of ownership scheme, including a large High Street chain that engages with its staff as 'partners' and shares the profits with them accordingly.

Sabbaticals — These are not currently statutory in the UK, but are proving popular in some high pressure professions, usually with key staff members. What about offering your most valuable employees up to six months' sabbatical as an option after a lengthy service period? Or even offering it connected to a key project with a forward deadline that has to be met? This might be a better option than them leaving, taking a break and joining a competitor. The sabbatical could be paid or unpaid leave, once the employee has reached ten years plus of service with your business as an example. They would have to apply for this option, and give you reasonable notice of when they intended to take their leave to enable you to organise suitable cover. If they left the company within two years of taking that sabbatical, they would agree to pay you back any salary taken whilst away (on a tapered scale, if you offered it as paid leave). There are many employees who would love to do some voluntary overseas work, but feel that they can only do it if they leave their employment. Or they just want to travel whilst they are still able to do so.

There are advantages to employers in their staff taking a sabbatical. The employee could learn a new language, get involved in politics, do some studying to improve themselves, such as the studying for an MBA, and even come back with a whole new view on your work and how things are done, because of the countries or places they have visited whilst travelling. Fresh thinking has to be — well — *fresh*!

Unlimited Leave

The reality of this option might be more achievable than an employer may first think from the headline.

In more recent (and some may argue enlightened) times some multi-nationals have started to offer their staff unlimited leave. This means that staff decide how much leave they require in the year, this can be from a couple of hours to a month on the understanding the employee will know how much time they need off, and when they think they can go without jeopardising the project or business.

The main reason this is being discussed by large organisations is to overcome 'presenteeism': low productivity of people who are physically present at work, however for various reasons are not contributing all that they could.

This type of leave policy (or lack of holiday policy) shows your employees that you trust them to make decision on their own, and that when the work is done, take your break. It has been compared to an all-you-can-eat buffet. The first few times you go, you eat until you can't physically eat any more, but as time goes on you eat only what you want and what you need.

If you as a business owner have the full understanding from your staff of your company goals, and the part they play in the organisation to reaching that goal, then this sort of scheme could be successful. I understand that the feedback so far from companies that have introduced unlimited leave is that it has been a success and that the system has not been abused.

As commented earlier in this book, there are a few people we know who are dropping out of work in their mid-forties and early fifties, due to burnout in some form, and this is a great way to retain these key employees, their wisdom of your business and to help with their future focus.

Burnout

Burnout is a common reason why employees leave. As a disruptor, do not forget you are asking a lot from them! This may well only be exacerbated by constant new, dynamic and creative thinking, possibly in areas that are not their natural habitat. It's true that this does create an exciting and dynamic environment to work in, but it is tiring all the same. Do we just relentlessly ask too much of individuals? There are various types of burnout: —

> ***Frenetic*** burnout is the stereotypical version, defined by workers who just have too much on their plate. These employees generally adopt a negative tone, and are sometimes found grumbling about their workload.

To help these individuals, you will need to find out if they are the only person who can do this work and what they feel is lacking to make them feel better valued. Do they need an assistant/machine capacity/budget/feedback? If they really do have too much on their plate, you as an employer may struggle to replace them as a vital member of the team if they were to leave. Be warned and be ready.

Under-challenged burnout, often not considered by many employers to be burnout as such. These are employees who plainly feel like they are not getting much satisfaction out of their work.

Possibly not as apparent as other forms of burnout, a team member experiencing this tends to 'cognitively avoid' their work, distancing themselves from what they consider an unrewarding experience. This behaviour is no use to you if you want full engagement in dynamic innovation, indeed it is almost the polar opposite. One concern is that this may pollute the more engaged members of your team and can be disruptive to your disruption plans. Motivate and train where you can, to engage, or even to re-engage, but recognise early if you have reached your limit with this identified position.

Worn-out employees struggle with the stress of the day-to-day workload and ultimately choose to neglect their work because of those pressures. The sabbatical option above springs to mind if you want to keep them in the long term.

These notes are generic and I am sure will seem a little simplistic to HR professionals. However, with innovation and disruption at the core of your conceptual progression, the task at hand and the workload associated with it are going to bring turbulence. Team members need to understand and absorb this concept, and possibly its personal outcomes. As an employer, be alert to the potential risks and help, train, provide where you can — although ultimately there will be casualties.

Remember the quote from Elon Musk: *"Failure is an option here. If things are not failing, you are not innovating enough."* I am sure he wasn't referring to team members in this context; however, in pressured, mind- and boundary-expanding situations, some human failure may be one cost that may not be apparent on the balance sheet, but can still have great detrimental effect.

Adding new members to the team as time demands grow is just as fraught, and finding time to recruit the right people is paramount. You do not want someone on your payroll whose success, limited or otherwise, is not a consequence of them being involved.

Recruitment

There is the phrase in many recruitment offices that *'an early bird catches the worm'*. However, this is not always the case in the motivational spectrum, because unhappy staff upload CVs to employment websites in the evening, and it is notable that if the recruitment consultant catches that CV before the individual goes to work the next day, they are likely to have a conversation together that will move that team member away.

If, as is possible, the CV was loaded in a fit of pique, there is a chance that your employee will change their mind once they are back at work and decide, at least for now, that they know where they are in their current role and that a change is not good for them at that point; or that they are just seeing whether they can improve their current remuneration. The 'better the devil you know' scenario may come into play here. The reality however is that they will only need their head turning one more time before they leave; and you may not want them on your team anyway.

Take your staff with you

It is great to be on a journey of discovery, as you break down barriers and overcome challenges to your disruptive project. You are likely to be asking a lot of yourself and those around you. Remember that they may find their own journey challenging. Make sure you take them with you in the process. It could be detrimental to everything if you don't.

Change communication

Another important point from my past business experience is that, when you make a change in your company, large or small, you must remember to think about how it will be received by the team. There are companies who charge a lot to manage business change; their magic ingredient is communication with staff.

I always like the misguided statement: *'I told you a thousand times!'* If you didn't understand it the first time, you won't understand the 999 other times either. The teller is the problem, not the receiver, so the message needs to be adjusted in order to get through.

Tell them, tell them and tell them again! And ensure you evolve along with them.

There are well documented historic studies of change and its effects: starting with the thought that people — your team — don't like change is probably not unreasonable, and then travelling through a range of varying emotions to reach integration, as follows: —

The Kübler-Ross change curve

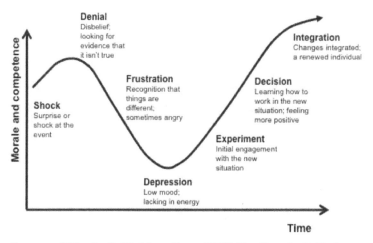

Source: Elisabeth Kubler- Ross 1973/On Death & Dying

Although this original diagram related to death and dying, many management studies have used this model in their research.

This process is natural and detailed further below. There are other views on the change process and we have added a further example (Vernon 1966) in Chapter Eight.

When you as a business owner/manager decide to implement a new scheme/plan/innovation — perhaps an office move, creating a new team, opening another office — then be ready for the stages that you might experience as feedback from team members.

Stage 1 — Shock

Surprise or shock at the event. The type of *"I can't believe they would do that"* chatter around the water fountain.

This is something to be watched, and addressed if there are concerns. Listening to these is key to being able to allay future discord.

Stage 2 — Denial

"They wouldn't do that!" This is when the reality of the planned change hits home, even if the change has been well planned and communicated. It's a bit like a tax hike announced by the Chancellor, but planned for the tax year eighteen months ahead. You know it's coming, even the detail, and then it 'suddenly' turns up in your payslip. Just like you, employees need time to adjust. Here, what your staff needs is information, to understand what is happening, and to know how to get help and guidance if needed.

This is a critical stage for communication. Make sure you communicate often, but also ensure that you don't overwhelm your staff. Employees need to know where to go for more information, so take the time to answer any questions that come up. *You* might understand, but if they don't, you have a problem.

Stage 3 — Resistance (anger, blame, defensiveness, frustration... all aimed at you as the boss!)

"There is no way I'm doing that!" As your staff start to react to the change, they may start to feel concern, anger, resentment or fear, especially if it is an office move to a new location. They may resist the change actively or passively. They may feel the need to express their feelings and concerns, and vent their anger with you or with others. This can be a critical time because it's when you start to find key staff leaving if you have not taken them along with you on the change journey.

Stage 4 — Depression

"This is a disaster!" For any organisation, this stage is a danger zone. Badly managed, the organisation or the project may descend into crisis.

As you would expect, this phase needs careful planning. You should prepare by carefully considering the impacts and objections that people may have, and endeavour to address them *before* they happen.

Complaining, open threats to quit...

Make sure you address these early with clear communication and support, and by taking action to minimise and mitigate the problems that people will experience. As the reaction to change is very personal, and can be deeply emotional, it is impossible to pre-empt every possible reaction. So, listen and watch carefully during this stage (or have mechanisms to help you do this) so you can respond to the unexpected.

Stage 5 — Experimenting, transition, letting go

This is the turning point for individuals and for the organisation. Once you turn the corner to Stage 5, the organisation starts to come out of the danger zone and is on the way to making a success of the changes.

Individually, as people's acceptance grows, they'll need to test and explore what the change means. They will do this more easily if they are helped and supported to do so; this may be a simple matter of allowing enough time.

Stage 6 — Decision, understanding (some optimism, some ideas)

As the person managing the changes, you can lay good foundations for this stage by making sure that people are well trained, and are given early opportunities to experience what the changes will bring.

Be aware that this stage is vital for learning and acceptance, and that it takes time; don't expect people to be fully productive during this time. Build in contingency time so that people can learn and explore without too much pressure.

Stage 7 — Integration, acceptance (commitment, enthusiasm, trust)

This stage is the one you have been waiting for! This is where the changes start to become second nature, and people embrace the improvements to the way they work.

As someone managing the change, you'll finally start to see the benefits you've worked so hard for. Your team or organisation starts to become productive and efficient and the positive effects of change become apparent.

Celebration

This part of any project, big or small, is vital.

While you are busy counting the benefits, don't forget to celebrate success! The journey may have been rocky, in fact *expected* to be rocky. Certainly it will have been at least uncomfortable for some people involved, as their routine thinking has been undone, tested, challenged and then rebuilt differently. It's a great but challenging process, not only for the concept but for the people involved. Recognise your team: everyone deserves to share the success. What's more, by celebrating the achievement you establish a track record of success which will make things easier the next time change is needed. This is a great way to cement the accomplishment of Stage 7 and the change process.

Remember the French Revolution. *'Let them eat cake'* in the reality of a modern celebration might be a good idea, but if it's gone wrong and your revolting staff believe you're thinking it in Marie Antoinette terms, you might find yourself in line for Madame Guillotine!

Scared of something different

Chapter Seven: Emotion

Emotion: *instinctive or intuitive feeling, as distinguished from reasoning or knowledge*

For me, the emotion of the innovation process and project management we undertook to make our product work stands out as one of the real costs of the project. I'm not sure even the word *rollercoaster* comes close to reflecting the chaos of emotions that you go through… over and over again. Angst, delight, anger, melancholy, fear, confusion, elation, excitement; they're all part of a good project, you just need to strap yourself in and hang on! Of any of the chapter definitions, I think this is one that could be easily overlooked and yet it is probably the most important in preparing to take a great concept through to delivery.

Thinking you are prepared is good. Being prepared is another thing entirely. It is also very important to prepare your loved ones for the journey you are about to embark on. You're about to expend a phenomenal amount of passion on something that is not them. They need to understand why you are doing it, its purpose, the task (along with its long hours) and what's in it for you. There may also be something ultimately in it for *them*.

This is how they understand and subsequently support you for the reward; it's human nature. So, before you read this chapter, answer that question: *Why are you doing this?*

If you don't yet know, don't start until you do. You will have no inner passion otherwise.

Emotions run deep

There are many emotions that you feel every day of your life. The emotions that you have at home and at work may well be different. Trying to plot the future path of possible emotions is not easy. Be ready for them all! There are many basic emotions such as greed, fear, love, ego and you can guess there are countless shades in between. For one thing, you must have had *some* ego to start your business all those years ago and to be starting a journey of disruption now.

If you were to think back to when you started any first enterprise, possibly your only business, can you remember the overriding emotion that pushed you to make the leap and start? I'm sure it was a big deal for you at the time; it certainly was for me. I remember it being a very anxious time, motivated largely by fear of the future. For me, the thought of remaining an employee who was mostly average is what made me do it. It wasn't the money I could earn as a business owner that spurred me on; it was the shackles of middle management restricting me that I felt were so pointless.

The unknown was beckoning and I often think about this as a motivator. That something so restrictive and profoundly negative to me at the time, namely being 'average', could drive me, with the help of my family, to do something so positive, that has become a beacon of stability and reliability for more than a decade, is inspiring. But why stop now? What was formerly the unknown can, in itself, become a comfort blanket. A decade later, it could be promoting the very 'averageness' you wanted to avoid. Possibly now not so negative, but probably restrictive in the longer term.

Right now, what's motivating *you*? Have you stopped to think about it? Many people feel they don't need to disrupt and make change. However, apathy could in itself be a challenge to your business. Do you care anymore? You have poured love, even passion into the fabric of your company, but do you still love it? It's very comfortable now but does it fire you up every morning; or, like the employee you may have once been, you attend it, it pays you money, you go home... done?

Answer these: —

- If you could change one thing in your company, what would it be?

- What's stopping you?

- Could you choose to make this change right now, even if it is just for your own wellbeing?

- What was the biggest achievement of your company, other than starting it?

- How did you celebrate?

- When will you do it next?

Can't answer them easily? You may know where you are already. Whatever you do, shake the tree of your business and see what falls out.

Natural progression through an awkward few years in your growth

Recently, a few calendar years have ended for our main business with successful income figures and firm single-digit growth figures, but a real feeling of lack of achievement to show for our efforts. Perhaps corporate memory will correct me in the future and identify this as merely natural business growing pains.

In reviewing this position, we were pleased with progress, determining that these 'graft' years are necessary to see continued growth and increased profitability in future times. We refer to the first decade as *the warm up act*. Re-investing into your business may feel unnatural when it's running well and is established, but if you want greater dividends later on, this is what is needed.

You might feel that this positive sentiment is welcome — but where to start?

Why not start with yourself? It's often a great starting point, although you should be aware that there may be some cognitive biases that challenge your decisions. I am delighted to have gained permission to reproduce the following **Business Insider document: *20 Cognitive Biases That Screw Up your Decisions***, which may help you with your planning and current mind set. To me, the diagram demonstrates the challenges you face in the processes of business decision making.

20 COGNITIVE BIASES THAT SCREW UP YOUR DECISIONS

1. Anchoring bias.

People are **over-reliant** on the first piece of information they hear. In a salary negotiation, whoever makes the first offer establishes a range of reasonable possibilities in each person's mind.

2. Availability heuristic.

People **overestimate the importance** of information that is available to them. A person might argue that smoking is not unhealthy because they know someone who lived to 100 and smoked three packs a day.

3. Bandwagon effect.

The probability of one person adopting a belief increases based on the number of people who hold that belief. This is a powerful form of **groupthink** and is reason why meetings are often unproductive.

4. Blind-spot bias.

Failing to recognize your own cognitive biases is a bias in itself. People notice cognitive and motivational biases much more in others than in themselves.

5. Choice-supportive bias.

When you choose something, you tend to feel positive about it, even if that **choice has flaws**. Like how you think your dog is awesome — even if it bites people every once in a while.

6. Clustering illusion.

This is the tendency to **see patterns in random events**. It is key to various gambling fallacies, like the idea that red is more or less likely to turn up on a roulette table after a string of reds.

7. Confirmation bias.

We tend to listen only to information that confirms our **preconceptions** — one of the many reasons it's so hard to have an intelligent conversation about climate change.

8. Conservatism bias.

Where people favor prior evidence over new evidence or information that has emerged. People were **slow to accept** that the Earth was round because they maintained their earlier understanding that the planet was flat.

9. Information bias.

The tendency to **seek information when it does not affect action**. More information is not always better. With less information, people can often make more accurate predictions.

10. Ostrich effect.

The decision to **ignore dangerous or negative information** by "burying" one's head in the sand, like an ostrich. Research suggests that investors check the value of their holdings significantly less often during bad markets.

11. Outcome bias.

Judging a decision based on the **outcome** — rather than how exactly the decision was made in the moment. Just because you won a lot in Vegas doesn't mean gambling your money was a smart decision.

12. Overconfidence.

Some of us are **too confident about our abilities**, and this causes us to take greater risks in our daily lives. Experts are more prone to this bias than laypeople, since they are more convinced that they are right.

13. Placebo effect.

When **simply believing** that something will have a certain effect on you causes it to have that effect. In medicine, people given fake pills often experience the same physiological effects as people given the real thing.

14. Pro-innovation bias.

When a proponent of an innovation tends to **overvalue its usefulness** and undervalue its limitations. Sound familiar, Silicon Valley?

15. Recency.

The tendency to weigh the **latest information** more heavily than older data. Investors often think the market will always look the way it looks today and make unwise decisions.

16. Salience.

Our tendency to focus on the **most easily recognizable features** of a person or concept. When you think about dying, you might worry about being mauled by a lion, as opposed to what is statistically more likely, like dying in a car accident.

17. Selective perception.

Allowing our expectations to **influence how we perceive** the world. An experiment involving a football game between students from two universities showed that one team saw the opposing team commit more infractions.

18. Stereotyping.

Expecting a group or person to have certain qualities without having real information about the person. It allows us to quickly identify strangers as friends or enemies, but people tend to **overuse and abuse** it.

19. Survivorship bias.

An error that comes from focusing only on surviving examples, causing us to **misjudge a situation**. For instance, we might think that being an entrepreneur is easy because we haven't heard of all those who failed.

20. Zero-risk bias.

Sociologists have found that **we love certainty** — even if it's counterproductive. Eliminating risk entirely means there is no chance of harm being caused.

SOURCES: Brain Biases; Ethics Unwrapped; Explorable; Harvard Magazine; HowStuffWorks; LearnVest; Outcome bias in decision evaluation, Journal of Personality and Social Psychology; Psychology Today; The Bias Blind Spot: Perceptions of Bias in Self Versus Others, Personality and Social Psychology Bulletin; The Cognitive Effects of Mass Communication, Theory and Research in Mass Communications; The less-is-more effect, Predictions and tests, Judgment and Decision Making; The New York Times; The Wall Street Journal; Wikipedia; You Are Not So Smart; ZhurnalyWiki

BUSINESS INSIDER

Doubt

Doubt is a common bedfellow of innovation and disruption. I'm not sure why this is; perhaps because creativity stretches the mind. I *do* know that you can regularly lose sleep when your mind is spinning as to whether your ideas will work.

I had not originally included the word *doubt* in this book, partly because the concepts I have been engaged with for our own business creation have been embraced with such confidence that doubt was, in principle, of little concern. The dictionary suggests the meaning to be '*to be uncertain about, consider questionable or unlikely, hesitate to believe*'. With these definitions noted, I think doubt should be embraced, because this is exactly what you are doing: taking what is uncertain... and then making it happen.

Next time you lie awake at night, wondering what really is going on, notepad at your side, know that you are in the right place. Doubt is your friend on this journey to a new solution and to defying convention. But when doubt visits you at 3.07AM, along with a possible solution, don't forget to note it down. You will not remember all its various aspects in the morning.

A trip to the 'bitter barn'

Occasionally, doubt itself will only be a short interlude; you'll hurtle past it on your way to experiencing frustration and eventually, possibly, a trip into what I call the 'bitter barn'. The bitter barn is where you find yourself when things get the better of you and start to grind you down, on the way to success. Negativity, distraction and fear can all be found in here, and will pin you down if you let them.

Never lose sight of the exit door. I do not feel that having a setback in a project or disruption process is a bad thing. Indeed, a setback can be turned into a positive thing because it tests resolve and even understanding. A setback makes you question why something is going wrong. It will annoy you and it will annoy others too. But being able to recognise and retreat from this position is vital, because if you allow it, a setback can be all consuming.

Innovation, disruption and change are challenging. The *verb* definition of change is '*make or become different*'. And you know this is not going to happen without some pain, self-doubt and the occasional gnashing of teeth.

Personally, I can find this dark side rewarding because it makes you look at things differently; negatively yes, but still differently. It is better for you to challenge yourself robustly than for someone else to enjoy doing it for you! This is a strength that needs to be engaged. It is better for you to discover faults, inconsistencies and problems yourself, than for them to be laundered in public after the launch of your new offering. You will not get it completely right first time. If your innovation is a *real* innovation, there will be nothing to judge it against. Build, produce and adjust — your journey does not end at production. That is only the start.

Just like the speeding journey past doubt, you also need to be able to speed through the 'bitter barn' and out the other side, using the experience to make a positive influence on your plans. The *noun* definition of change is '*an act or process through which something becomes different*'. Well, that's what you're all about! Just make sure you know where your line of travel is and will be; stopping can be toxic, know that there are going to be tricky stages along the way and most of all be prepared to take the journey. It will be worth it.

Of course, you might want to beat yourself up about something that happened, or didn't happen, or some point that was missed — or, or, or! As you might guess, it's possible to go round the houses many times if you get too close to the computer screen to be able to see what's on the screen. I appreciate that this idea glides un-worryingly across the page as you read it here; believe me, when you face the issue for real it won't do that. Unless you can detach from the issue and view it objectively, you will find it takes a lot longer to resolve than to read about it.

In decades past, you would have left your desk at this point for a cigarette break. In this new politically correct and healthier world, this is a disagreeable pastime. Even the new vaping systems are frowned upon, even though this in itself is an innovation. A trip to the gym after work and running for twenty minutes on the treadmill or swimming twenty lengths of the local pool is a great, and better, way to clear your mind. I jest that it pushes the cholesterol around the body a bit further, but the reality is that it does help the mind with its search for solutions. It is often best to clear your mind before you go home, rather than take it out on those you love.

Fancy a snooze?

The project and I have both benefitted from 'sleeping on it' for twenty-four hours, effectively maturing any response or action that is required. Build time into your planning model to allow for this. That extra day has great value as long as you can afford the time, and I know from experience that this is not always the case.

Rumi, the thirteenth century poet and theologian, suggests two quotes that will help you find the exit if needed. These are: —

"What you seek is seeking you,"

and also,

"Stop acting so small. You are the universe in ecstatic motion."

Wise words indeed. If you struggle to get in and out of the dark side/bitter barn, whatever you choose to call it, share it with others in the project and enlist them to pull you out. You will be sharing the glory when it works, so share some of the pain as well. You also know when to pull others out of their own struggles, so it is not unreasonable to ask the same of them.

Personal wellbeing

I hope you are still engaged with your business and innovation, both in mind and spirit. Attitude is everything. Without engagement, spirit, drive, determination *and* enjoyment, it's not going to happen. If you don't enjoy what you do, each day drags. I know I am engaged and, as I head towards the age of fifty, I am delighted to have maintained the enthusiasm for business, even after these intense revolutionary years.

When you are fully immersed in the business's needs and requirements, it is easy to forget about your own personal well-being, fitness, health and family. As the recession hit and while it meandered through our slowing global economy, many business owners needed to rely on their personal determination and grit to steer the business they had created through these choppy waters and into the safe haven beyond. Well done to them, but it has been challenging and required an entirely different way of thinking. Once you get into this mindset it is very easy not to let go and to forget to relax a little now and then… if business and profits allow of course!

Move with the changing economy and business market and embrace change and opportunity when available, managing this accordingly. As a cautionary tale, there was a period of time post-recession when some American CEOs had to be retrained in order to stop them continuing to cut costs and to refocus on more positive reinvestment and growth to build their respective businesses back up.

The website, TechWhirl.com, featured an article about this by LavaCon Perspectives: ***Stop Cutting Costs. Start Enhancing Revenue*** in its issue in November 2014. It's well worth a read to consider the fundamental problems with just a cost-cutting approach.

The ***Harvard Business Review*** focused on this topic in September 2014, in its article ***Profits without Prosperity*** by William Lazonick and it is recommended reading.

Running out of steam

Running out of steam is a real issue that needs to be monitored in the delivery of your innovation. You're being challenged all the time and this in itself is, well… challenging. Project planning takes time anyway and it is a far easier process when there is a well-trodden path and little conceptual innovation. When you are innovating there is little or no path to follow, which creates extra pressure... and excitement! No one will have built before what you are building, and your research may push you down a particular line, but you are still the icebreaker across a frozen business sea, creating a channel for others to follow. Most likely they are already watching, if not catching you up, hoping to overtake you — but you are still the new market maker.

Be aware of this additional potential burden and build extra personal reserves into the journey, to allow you and your colleagues to deal with the dead ends and false starts you may encounter. These are exhilarating, inspirational times. Thrive on them by all means, but always keep extra energy ready. The two years that the team and I have worked on the development, testing, launch and first year programme of our project have been some of the most stressful we have endured. Stressful in many cases in a positive way — but still stressful.

The answer is behind you

I appreciate that this sub-heading is contrary to the subheading in Chapter Four, Construction: *The answer is not behind you — look ahead!* But an observation, or even a solution from the past, can be an alternative.

Coming up with a good business idea or application that could gain traction to innovate within your business is not the easiest of things. If it were we would all be doing it. Well, it isn't. You are a trail blazer.

Creativity and innovation are two very different things. Having the imagination to go past what counts as creativity, to *innovate,* is something that does not come naturally to many of us. Searching for a new solution may not be the easiest path to success. We often consider what has gone in the past to provide us with a guide to what could be achieved in the future. As a business leader, you will have suffered frustration in your progresses through your business success. These 'pinch points', as I call them, are issues that should not be part of your business, but they do exist and they slow down innovation, production and success. It is good to think of them as a challenging opportunity rather than a persistent problem, if you can.

WD-40, the penetrating oil, was invented by Norman Larsen in 1953. The '40' part stands for the fortieth formula because it was Larsen's fortieth attempt to perfect and create his Water Displacement solution. So, when *you* reach a pinch-point and start your search for an ideal solution, do not lose faith in your innovation. It may take you many tries before you perfect it.

Turning the position on its head, conundrums and challenges are almost the disruption you are seeking in themselves — but possibly not in a good form. How can this negative position be flipped to a positive and profitable outcome? You may have overcome these immediate issues at the time — but they usually prey on your mind, and you will be motivated to ensure that they don't crop up again.

So, what caused these issues? Was it you, or was it the system? If it was the system, how can you streamline it for the future? And if you could streamline it, what would be the potential outcome? If you could create an alternative solution to the situation, what else would you include or exclude within your plan to centralise a new solution?

Could this idea or solution then be commoditised for you, your colleagues, your business, your industry or profession, who could then use it to turn current practices on their head?

Think about it. Looking back at your knowledge and experience can often provide you with the start point to the way forward. In part, it did for us. We felt that our industry's face-to-face advice process was somewhat clunky and labour-intensive. It has been dominant in UK advice provision for decades without challenge. However, suitable technology has rarely been in place to be applied to the process to create an alternative. Many would argue that the financial services business is all about people and relationships; I am not convinced that this model will be the only real option in the future. With the evolution in technology, and especially fintech, demand for non-face-to-face solutions continues to grow. The concept lends itself well to lower costs for advice and implementation to the end user. This is also attractive in creating volumes and building market share.

We have also encompassed a lighter, younger writing style and graphic process, colours and ethos to our new offering compared to that of our main, more technical, possibly 'heavier' core offering. I have enjoyed this variation, having tested it on a group of people from a local company we work with. We would offer to help them test new ideas if they asked. Being able to call on their 'general public' expertise and opinion is invaluable.

Think about this when you plan your approach to your new offering. Who, as independent neutral observers, could help you as testers and friendly critics?

The final personal push?

Personally, I am fearful of age. As I write these words, I am forty-eight years old. I still have the business fire in my belly to drive, disrupt and innovate our business forward. This determination is a powerful ally for growing, creating, inspiring myself and others to deliver. I fear that in five years' time, I might not have this energising and enjoyable desire, and will at that time ignore most of my own good advice in this book and just want to coast into my future. Feel free to remind me of this in five or six years' time. I appreciate that time will dictate whether the work we have undertaken is enough.

I also know that, at this time of real business revolution and evolution, I have not done everything I believe I can achieve, nor reached the heights I aspire to. Daunting and thrilling at the same time, with challenging tasks ahead, to me this is what to me innovation is all about. As you will see, we have planted some seeds, through innovation and process disruption in our online business, to help towards this target in six or so years' time.

Do you think you could do more? Have you stopped asking 'what if?' and are you now accepting what your working life has turned out to be? For me, and most of my team, the last two years' programme of achieving our innovative project, at the same time as continuing to serve the demands of our main business, has been gruelling. Laying down the foundations of your new plans, alongside your main business or as a separate entity, it all needs to be mapped, challenged, integrated, managed and implemented — with, in our case, our core business supporting the innovation.

I have personally thrived because of it. The timing of this creative push has been vital, to create the branded platform to reach new heights by the time that notional five-year deadline is up. There is no real business logic in this, but I find it useful to set down personal parameters like these, so I can tell whether each point is being met at the correct time.

This does not mean that my colleagues and I will be finished by the age of fifty-five. Probably we'll feel as if we've just got going, with our best years yet to come. However, I do want our new proposition to be complete, developed, launched, evolved and matured by this time. That's a lot to ask but if we focus and maintain passion we can do it.

With *my* personal challenges noted, what about yours? What is it and in what time will your innovation have reached its maturity? You will need to know this to deliver the outcomes you want.

Scared of something different

Chapter Eight: Disruption

Disruption: *disturbance or problems which interrupt an event, activity or process*

Writing about disruption is challenging — because it *is* disruptive! Disruption has no respect for barriers, rules and guidelines. It is unruly and troublesome and at the same time joyous, even ebullient, in the way it can transform. This next chapter was challenging to write and it may be challenging to read. I make no apology for this because it is challenging *you* to make a difference, as we have.

In my own journey of discovery, I have caused some people a good deal of upset. I am proud of this — not because I have upset people but because, if my project is causing so much consternation, it must be seen as a threat, and this in itself is some validation of its potential. We have created an opportunity to disrupt their business. That wasn't on our agenda at the outset, although the upheaval of the standard model certainly was a core focus. It would be fair to say that the two are the same. Observed by our peers, some positively engaging and, of course, some detracting, even our profession's press noted the potential disruptive influence of our innovation.

When you think about all those annoying moments that no boss or exam paper can teach you and all those quick wins, they are the 'highs' of being in your profession that showed you which way to turn and more vitally, which way to avoid. With this wisdom comes responsibility. That's nothing new, of course. But it also provides the opportunity for new thinking, using modern techniques to disturb traditional models with the objective of gaining future advantage.

Evolution in real terms remains a controversial idea for some people. However, in business terms it should be positively embraced. You may prefer to call this process *adaptation* and that's fine. It might be innovation or even disruption. They are all good!

The concept of turning the past on its head is not new. This has been advocated often enough before and there are some great books to help inspire you.

One book I read some years back was *'Flip: How to Turn Everything You Know on Its Head'* by Peter Sheahan. It's well worth a read if you have the chance.

As the title suggests, Sheahan looks at business and the opportunity to flip it on its head and see what happens. Possibly one of the first modern era business disruptors, the book was published in 2007 in Australia, at a time when the internet and social media were in their infancy. Using the principle of disruption, I wonder what the content would look like now if it were brought up to date with the advances in technology achieved since then, and those which seem likely to happen in the next few years. As Sheahan suggests in the opening text, it's all about *"...taking a risk and putting it all on the line. Keep your nerve!"*

The Disruptor

I recently wrote an article for Citywire on the topic of disruption. They published this, but gave it the title, *The Disruptor*. What a thrill to be cited by CityWire as the man who is shaking up my profession to catapult it into the twenty-first century. That's praise indeed. The dark nights of writing in November 2015 for me suddenly seemed worthwhile, as we continued the further development of our project.

Do you, as a much needed disruptor of your profession or industry, want to do the same thing in your specialist area: break the principles and rules as your sector emerges into the fourth industrial revolution.

Never stand still

To me, one of the most important issues is the pace of change. 'Never stand still' is becoming a new mantra because, in the process of disruption, it is easy to stop and marvel at what is being achieved; but that to me is where the disruption stops. That's the time to grab your virtual coat and go in search of the *next* phase, development or disruption. Be prepared for everything and nothing. Rome wasn't built in a day and in real life you need to be aware of the accumulation of small gains as you continually move forward.

Let me give you an example. Providing good financial services advice has always been about questioning, understanding, getting under the skin of the client, challenging opinions, attitudes and asking *why?* — and then you keep on challenging until you know the clients real underlying needs and objectives. And, in both scenarios of advice and disruption, if you stop too early you are unlikely to reach the real answers.

Planning your path carefully, but with no pre-determined end, will bring you to the best possible solution. The outcome will evolve in front of you, a shared journey, and the project itself will tell you when it's reached its natural end, rather than you deciding.

Make sure your new offering, virtual or physical, is the best you can get it to be, or delay any launch until you are ready for scrutiny. The urge to push forward, to develop, to improve, is always there, but if you manage to stay objective you will simply *know* when it's time.

My passion to innovate makes me very proud, and I think I'm a better person because of it. This passion has challenged my deep-seated habitual thinking on how to make things happen. With new technology and methods, this no longer has to be the case. The time is right to disrupt whoever you are, to step away from the crowd, to look at where they're heading and ask *why there? why them? is this route efficient?* You begin to see that if the crowd would all head your way, they would find things a lot simpler, quicker, efficient, cheaper — and just better.

More importantly, how are you going to disrupt your own business methods and that of your competitors? I urge you to step out of your crowd right now. As I will say at the end of this book, no one is going to thank you for turning their world upside down. Quite the contrary, they are more likely to query why you are upsetting the apple cart that has served them so adequately for years. Well, the cart is tired and so is their thinking — and that is not going to stop you making change happen.

To look at this position in another, more positive way, Ronald Reagan is quoted as saying: —

'There is no limit to the amount of good you can do if you don't care who gets the credit.'

I appreciate that you will care who gets the credit, but he also said:

'There are no great limits to growth because there are no limits of human intelligence, imagination, and wonder.'

True disruption is a lonely place to be, but thinking differently from the rest of the crowd always has been. And if you are an advocate of innovation and disruption, you can probably trace this personal, and beneficial, trait all the way back throughout your life. You probably used to wonder why your parents and teachers would reprimand you for not conforming.

You're not the only one, not then and not now. These are the forward thinkers and influencers, unshackled from limitations and habitual perception. Just make sure you mix with those people, and share their desires and enthusiasm, whenever you can.

Disruptors' forum

Having recently met with a group of disruptors in a hugely energised forum in London, it is clear to me that that any new concept, innovation or idea is not about you, it's about the end user. That's who will always have the final say, in how they use your service, and usually not in the way you anticipated. This thought takes me back to the saying 'the customer is always right'. That is correct, but in this case, instead of just the individual purchase, it's also the way your offering prospers, evolves and develops.

In this forum I was struck by how willing each member of the panel was to share, on camera and off-air, what they had achieved so far and where they were heading. The theme for us all was similar, but each one of us had found our own route to subtly different answers to what was broadly the same question. With great respect to all involved, I could compare it to kids in a playground after Christmas, wanting to tell each other what toys they'd got. Refreshingly, there were no stuffed shirts and I think this was a testament to their total immersion in the quest to make a real positive difference. I thoroughly enjoyed the engagement.

'On-Boarding' costs

Each concept and final delivery option will have a different 'on-boarding' cost, with face-to-face or human interaction usually being the most labour intensive and therefore the most expensive of these to distribute. Human interaction also introduces the risk, where applicable, of compliance/ technical failure in delivering any complex outcomes. UK financial services are an obvious example where process and compliance are, in part, a requirement of the outcome — and if either of these is incorrect, it can leave the provider open to complaints, costs and redress.

You only have to think about the UK Payment Protection Insurance (PPI) debacle. The verdict was that the product was systematically mis-sold by the providers through their chosen distribution channel of sales teams in branch; this, I believe, may be partly part why the banks pulled out of the retail financial advice sector around 2012.

Whatever line of business you are in, the option to go direct-to-client ('D2C') is, through low-cost technology, universally available and, in my opinion, a great way of keeping the larger corporations honest as they are disrupted by new concepts and products from SMEs. There are development costs and the pressures of management time and, as the chief executive of one PLC reminded me after noting a few frustrations, *Rome was not built in a day*. He was not amused when I suggested that the Romans should have used the internet; it would have been far quicker! However, his sentiment was correct, and was reaffirmed at this disruptors' forum: it takes many months, even years, to gain momentum and to channel the user energy and feedback to gain traction, success and profit. This is easy to lose sight of when you are post-innovation and into production.

We have all seen small operations, often in their infancy, bringing great new ideas to their industry — only to be consumed by larger groups wishing to add that same dynamism to their own existing propositions.

Online facilities are, at the other end of the 'on-boarding' provision cost spectrum, streamlining and complying offerings, standardising volume outcomes and keeping technical compliance costs to a minimum. Maintaining service and time standards, with minimum human interaction, is an attractive proposition. Revisiting output standards is far easier on your own terms, than it is to react to negative feedback from outside sources. Indeed, the sales volumes that a system can provide are inspiring and let you sleep at night — for the most part — reassuring you that, as long as the programming is correct, future issues will be kept to a minimum. This is not always the case, as we have seen with the growing number of car recalls in recent years, mainly due to safety issues, as examples.

Find your fellow disruptors and share, within limits, your plans and thoughts. Listen to them. I have often found that a throwaway line can be powerful and positive in a 'what did they mean by that?' way. Let your intelligence apply itself to what you are achieving. Who are they using as resources? What value do they gain from this? Could these technology advocates add value to *your* project?

It's not all about you

Part of the purpose of this book is to challenge your current thinking about your existing business and the paths that it uses to achieve its outcomes and success. You need to climb off your current business 'apple cart' to see where it's really heading and why.

What have you really built? And has it built trust with the end user? Trust by the end user is vital. Without it you will not build usage, sales and of course profitable success.

Indeed, you need to check periodically what you mean by success. Are the results that you are currently returning real success, or just mediocrity? Do they push the boundaries of where you could be? And success does not necessarily mean income or profit. It can mean whatever you want it to be. It could be quality of life, by gaining time whilst achieving the same income level. Time is a hugely under-valued resource. So, what is your real quest?

I have noted in previous books that there are only two real ways to improve profits: improve income (sales) or reduce costs. Some accountants may chuckle at this admittedly simplistic observation — but as the driver of the business, these are the key points you can influence. The obvious utopian solution for profit is to do both. The mission of improved use of technology may be one way to do this. Be ready. The laws of foreseen and unforeseen consequences may be at their most apparent at this time, possibly including job losses if you can create efficiencies, but progress will stop for no one. The reference to China's economy made this point in the first chapter.

If you contract out work to third parties to help with your objectives, and I am sure you do, then when is the last time you reviewed the services they offer you? We have found over the final years of our first decade of business that some of these providers have not moved on as our business has, embracing technology. In reality, the initial contract that was established to meet our needs at the start no longer reflects our current larger trading style and volumes. Also, their use of technology updates and innovation has not been proactive in helping further to improve our service, in efficiencies of cost or service. On review and negotiation of terms, their progressive view had stalled, whilst our company was still on a journey forward. I am very pleased to note our continued progress, but this needs to be reflected in *every* aspect of our services.

Do you still extract full value from your contracted-out services now, as you did at the start? Knowing how technology can bring innovative advances in the way services can now be used, could the real value of the service be replaced by technology?

Taking an objective look at our own current face-to-face traditional service, we realised that for the mainstream consumer the answer is *yes*. For our traditional business model, the ordinary person in the street is not our *main* company's typical target. Therefore, the real answer in the longer term, and by this I mean the next decade, is that both the old and the new solutions we offer will need to maintain value; the former while it enters its maturity-phase descent curve, and the new solution in its infancy. This follows the mantra of 'never stand still'. If you can see a potential decline in a business model, but not its end use, this is the opportunity to disrupt, to innovate, but to deliver and start the infancy process again.

We have moved around 80% of our outsourced business contracts in the last two years in order to 'upgrade' the service we receive, and to match our changing objectives more closely. The benefits are significant. Costs have remained largely unchanged or even reduced. Where technology has been able to replace physical services we have achieved this, admittedly with some important and additional investment into our infrastructure as we grow. What these new services enable us to offer has increased and this has, unsurprisingly, added greater confidence to the team. In each case, with planning, the implementation proved fairly straightforward, although team briefings and communications were vital to ensure all made the journey with us.

Importantly, the services being provided now reflect our business more accurately, including the ability to expand further in the next phase of our plans.

New relationships and one night stands

My experience of disrupting the existing model we use has provided many opportunities to work with new people and contacts with whom I would otherwise never have engaged before. These forward thinkers are inspiring and

I would recommend that if you can join a group, either personally or through social media as examples, this should be worthwhile in pushing your plans forward. Don't anticipate an easy ride though. Disrupting and challenging existing models is a lonely business, as is running any business. Some contacts may fizzle out before they even really get going. However, others, as I found at the disruptors' forum, will be well worth the time and will move you on.

Reflect on your encounters and encourage those you want to work with, collaborating where you can.

Collaboration

How far could you take your outsourcing? I know you are not alone in wanting to extract part of your business and hand it to a third party to enable you to focus on other issues. Could this in itself be an opportunity to collaborate with other like-minded companies to create an individual product or service that could be sold to others, without giving away intellectual property to any greater extent? Perhaps the application of some inter-operability of systems between groups of organisations with a mission to solve a historic, or unprofitable element, section of production may be appropriate?

Think about it:

- What do you outsource and why?

- Do others need, or might they value, this service or product?

- Would they pay for it if it were packaged, and if so how much would they pay?

- Who could you collaborate with to create this new opportunity, sharing the development costs and, of course, the future profits, either as income or the sale of this hybrid business?

The opportunities might be already staring you in the face, although life (and innovation, for that matter) is usually not that straightforward. Whatever you do, just take another look. If there is a way of creating a new profitable venture, take it, before someone else beats you to it. Experiment with what could be created and then discuss it with your team.

Buying-in talent

In previous business books I have written, I've always advocated the challenge of *'are you the person for the job'*? By this, I mean that if you have a project, task, or target, ask yourself whether you are the best person to achieve this, or could you delegate it to another person, either inside or outside your business. I am an advocate of outsourcing, because others are likely to have an entirely different view of your profession, product or service, and will hopefully bring fresh thinking. And if they don't, of course, you can end the contract.

An alternative to this, if budgets allow, is to buy-in focused talent from outside which will meet your needs and objectives. They can be added in specifically for the project at hand, or as a full team member. The advantage of this again is fresh thinking for an innovation or project, and bringing a different feel to a new product, using expertise gained from other markets or applications. As a business, we found we were keen to bring a completely different outlook to our new product. Not that there was anything wrong with the existing service, we just wanted it focusing in a different direction in terms of delivery and target audience. However, we also felt that our SME budget could go further, gaining more traction more quickly, by using the outsource solution and technology alternatives where possible.

For example, many university programmes have innovation hubs, along with Business Angel funding in most cases, who are looking for the next big thing. This might be a worthwhile prospect if you are looking for alternative solutions. At the very least, it will show you what other industries are achieving in changing their world, and some of their ideas could be applied to your plans.

Both outsourcing and buying-in talent may give different outcomes, and certainly different budget costs. Outsourcing may be cheaper but with front-loading of costs. Control may also be forfeited, to some extent, on the timings of delivery, so strict application is required. Buying in talent may have a greater overall cost, although this is likely to be spread over time and you will keep control of timings.

The end of your business 'bucket list'? ... NEVER stand still!

Have you ever reached a stage in your life where, for whatever reason, you began to feel that you had nothing else to achieve? It might be a big birthday, or recognition by your peers, an award, or a higher qualification, even an anniversary that makes you pause and reflect. In business, these 'thought harbours' can be rare. This is understandable when you take into account the pressure that most of us are under.

For me, it was a combination of things crossing over that made me stop. In reality, it was not that I had nothing else to achieve, but a few milestones coincided. My wife celebrated a big birthday, I passed thirty years in my profession, our new business innovation celebrated its first anniversary, I was awarded Chartered status and a Fellowship… for the second time… and the company clicked over its eleventh year of profitable trading. There was much to celebrate, and to consider, condensed into a three-month period. It felt like more than I had imagined I would ever achieve in my working career, like the 'bucket list' of things to do before you retire, but business related. If you had a bucket list of ten life objectives and you achieved them all, would you just collect a gold watch and leave, mission complete, or think up ten more ideas?

Or, if you could do it all again in the era of the Fourth Industrial Revolution, how much better would it be? Quicker, more profitable, less exhausting… the list is endless… and so inspiring! Remember 'NEVER stand still!' Would the reality be that any second 'top ten' list would be even more adventurous than the first? Probably it would, as you push yourself on to greater things. It's only natural. And if you have not yet finished that first 'top ten' list and prepared the second, would you *replace* the remaining plans with the new ones? If so, go for it!

For me, the new and dynamic online financial advice project we have been developing has been a real inspiration and motivator. Part of *my* bucket list is to prove that this online proposition is the future and that it can disrupt an existing model.

Real environmental advantages... and savings!

Innovation in any existing process and its delivery within a new model cannot fail to use new technology to improve its user experience, usually reducing costs for both you and the consumer. You would probably not undertake the process if this were not likely to be an outcome. You'd also expect to improve profits, and this is nothing that you did not already know. The end result may be a full or partial online service or experience, without the need for meetings or staff to service the proposition. It's not such a far cry from the click-and-delivery systems so many of us use to buy groceries.

One additional major advantage, and often *not* a motivator for the original planning, is the reduction in environmental impact that the new delivery is likely to have over the existing model or system once technology is introduced. If you are reading this book on an e-reader this a great case in point. No printing production, so lower cost of production and lower cost of natural resources (such as pulp to make paper), and electronic distribution direct to the end user rather than physical transport and packaging.

When we look at our existing professional services model and the way we engage, advise and complete work for clients, we usually have two meetings in our High Street offices, plus telephone calls, and drive to and from the office to service these meetings. Add to this the day to day office running costs and staff costs, headed paper, even the cost of toilet paper! The list is endless and I appreciate that in reality not all of these costs could or would reduce. The investment in technical infrastructure to achieve the new delivery systems may cause costs to go up, with the potential later of having to lay off staff as and when their role becomes digitised. Financially, it amounts to a front-loaded business plan, with the added potential for some real environmental savings. Accountants might cringe at this outdated principle of front loading; however, we often say that the business answer is behind you. This model might work with the right cash flow modelling, and these need to be carefully crafted.

If you have not considered this before, it is a worthwhile process, possibly leading to a key selling point/advantage over the existing competition. There is much over-use of the 'green' ticket, and sadly, as we have seen with certain motor manufacturers, over-emphasis on the *published* environmental and economic benefits, whereas the reality may be very different. This only serves to create mistrust both within the company concerned, and also in the wider industry, about the statements of any green credentials. However, this is a vital issue for everyone and we are all involved, whether we choose to be or not. Carbon emissions are recognised globally as a massive and growing problem, and we believe that business is a great starting point when it comes to reducing them. We believe that our new entity, SaidSo.co.uk, for example, achieves carbon reductions by cutting the need for meetings and physical paperwork. I would thoroughly recommend engaging with an organisation such as Planet First to join 'The Planet Mark' programme. More detail can be found in the resources section at the end of this book.

Could *your* new enterprise do the same? Taking this a step further, could this be your new innovation? It would still be your product... but online, more functional and more environmentally friendly. Leave no stone unturned in challenging existing thinking.

I asked myself this a year ago: '*Are* there any stones unturned?' There were — and I am still turning over stones today. The business and our innovation are far the better for it. Never fear disruption or change. I, and our businesses, are vigorous supporters of both. Change is good, whatever form it takes, and in whatever generation history illustrates it.

The punk generation!

Many people do not fear *change* at all. All they 'fear' is the unknown, and to some extent this is a natural response.

When we started our first company there was no fear of change; my personal and business lives had been full of it at the time. It could be suggested that the idea behind starting the company was to slow down *future* change. Forward thinking? Maybe! Change had almost become part of the adventure of making it to the end of the working day. But the decision to make that leap into the unknown was a big issue.

Our business model at the time was not especially innovative, although this dynamism accelerated as we progressed, but it felt like a major change, and I am pleased we made it. Innovating always involves a leap of faith, but if you believe in your plans, this should turn out to be more fun than terrifying. I urge you to go for it and remember: failure is an option.

Speaking of fear, Malcolm McLaren, the late impresario and manager of the Sex Pistols, and who was an all-round provocative master of thinking differently, said: —

"What matters is this: being fearless of failure arms you to break the rules. In doing so, you may change the culture and just possibly, for a moment, change life itself."

He also said: —

"I was taught that to create anything you had to believe in failure, simply because you had to be prepared to go through an idea without any fear. Failure, you learned, as I did in art school, to be a wonderful thing. It allowed you to get up in the morning and take the pillow off your head."

The Sex Pistols were certainly not a failure of their time, either at launch or subsequently. After all, Mr McLaren was a tenacious and controversial business manager, but that's what the era needed — different thinking. And if that upset people, so be it.

Punk was an attitude, rather than just music or fashion. But were the Sex Pistols a disruptor of their time? Or perhaps just a persuader? They were certainly different: new, noisy, full of attitude and energy, and preying on fear of the degradation of the fabric of society. They did leave a legacy, but as time has passed, I find myself wondering now: were they genuinely *innovative*? Probably not. But they removed all the perceived barriers regarding how far you could go in the music.

And let's not forget the fashion industry of the time, with the world becoming a little less innocent in the course of that cleverly-engineered process. McLaren certainly headed the cultural change curve at that time. Whatever their effects, the Sex Pistols certainly were not 'scared of something different'.

'Johnny Rotten' (John Lydon) in his autobiography of 2014, *'Anger is an Energy'*, details his unique journey during the turbulent time of youth culture in the 1970s. I couldn't agree more with the title; anger really is an energy and one that needs to be captured when facing the challenges of innovation. Channelled well, anger is of real value — and of course, when used incorrectly, it's destructive both at the point of its deployment and into the longer term.

Was punk itself the innovation and disruptor? Embracing a new culture as a whole — its music, its clothes, its attitude — was that a trend that changed the world? Rather than an individual, such as Malcolm McLaren, influencing a cause, an entire group? It was certainly a two-fingered salute to 'more of the same'.

Reflecting on your new work, is the project and innovation that you are striving to achieve the new 'punk' culture of our modern generation? McLaren said: *"I've always thought that gaming and YouTube and the web is a very post-punk extravaganza."*

Think about it: we are in uniquely revolutionary times. You are unlikely to get another opportunity like it. The change curve is alive and well and, most importantly, still curving. You probably know what this feels like, as illustrated below using the International Product Lifecycle model from the American economist Raymond Vernon (1966) / Proven Models:

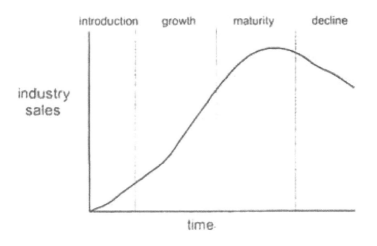

Source: Product Life-cycle theory / Raymond Vernon / First published 1966

What role are you playing in changing the same-old same-old? Remember that, when you're ready, you'll need to pump it out loud, just like the Sex Pistols, to ensure that you capture the imagination of your audience.

Press time

Allowing yourself time to answer press enquires and questions, issue press releases, marketing teasers and to address interest from third parties is important. It is easy to regard these as a nuisance when you don't want to give away too much information, part way through your plans, but the press can be a powerful ally when you want to get your message out. Work with them and they will work for you.

Make sure you know where you are on your planned change curve. For real innovation and disruption, you are the pace-setter and have some control of the curve.

Then you can ensure that you are at the right point in the change process for your innovation.

This interest and opportunity will not last forever.

Scared of something different

Chapter Nine: Conclusion

Conclusion: *a judgement or decision reached by reasoning*

Where do I start? Innovation and disruption are such stimulating subjects. The power of the internet as a distribution model empowers us all to make a big difference. It's just a question of how we go about it.

Where does your opportunity or project start to make this difference, which will change the lives of you, your staff and your company for years ahead? It starts deep in your mind and its unbridled imagination. You can create havoc, disruption and something altogether inspirational and new.

The conclusion of this book is proving to be the toughest part to write. Is there ever a real conclusion to innovation? The creative truth is that there is not — and that's what makes it so dynamic, not to mention addictive. The human mind's wheels of imagination, experimentation, disruption, ideas and delivery will never stop as long as the cerebral function continues to be nourished. This in itself is an exciting prospect; it's what makes the world change every second of every day.

Rules are there to be re-written and defied and then broken. The evolution of what we do and how we do it is always changing, diversifying, and hopefully being improved upon. No one will thank you for your work and innovation, but you did not start your new disruptive plans in the hope of thanks. You started your journey all those weeks, months and years ago with the intention of making a difference, and of course you hoped to be profitable in the process.

Both are only natural desires. I hope you more than achieved them, or on the way to and can stand proud not only of the final result, but also of the journey itself.

I also hope that in reading through the pages of *Scared of Something Different*, a few points have pricked your mind into realising that your mission is not complete and you are not yet heading for the final chapter. Irrespective of your business type, size or service, where are you on the journey?

Your next chapter is ready to be written. You have the touch-pad — start writing!

Your timing is going to be key, and delivery of the launch even more so. You will not get everything — product, service, widget, system — perfect. Perfection is a laudable goal, but it is nothing without delivery. Indeed, 'perfection' does not exist, but a stage completion does. And even if it did, it would only be perfect at one point in time, until someone, hopefully you, innovate past that point to achieve something even better. This can also happen because other non-related innovations and inventions come along and overlap with your sector. It is an exciting time to be involved and a real opportunity to make a mark on the world. In years to come the history books will confirm that this connected and innovative era will not be repeated again for another century or so.

Your new personal revolution!

Many people already know that we're privileged to be innovating and creating at this time. Like the Industrial Revolution of a century ago, this time is our opportunity to change things. Changing the world now is not restricted to the landed gentry and wealthy landowners of the 1800s. The World Economic Forum in January 2016 spoke of the Fourth Industrial Revolution, and that is exactly what we are experiencing right now. The possibilities to a person with power to their computer are restricted only by their wisdom and imagination. What an awesome prospect! We all need to stop the rhetoric and see what we can bring to the new revolution.

Disruption is your friend and the old ways, in all walks of life, although tried and tested, can now be improved upon with the new thinking and resources we have available to us. Our connected lives have already changed beyond all imagination, but we are only at the start. Mobile connectivity will bring us even greater opportunities, collective thinking, cleverer services and applications, simpler processes, lower carbon emissions, and hopefully a better, easier and more enjoyable world.

You will make mistakes, it's inevitable, and you just need to be ready for these personal, testing setbacks. Be reassured these are natural growing pains and there will also be successes and results that will surpass your expectations, however massive you planned them to be. We, as a team, have endured and enjoyed both experiences and are better people because of the journey. Remember, it *is* a journey; one that will take from you personally as you give your all to your project success.

You give of yourself every day of the week to ensure that your business functions, so this is going to be an extra 'ask' over and above your daily routine. Ensure that the final result also gives back to you, so that the personal sacrifice you put in is amply rewarded with personal satisfaction.

Don't forget that this is an opportunity and that real opportunities do not come along that often. When they are created by you, there is nothing to fear from their success.

Fear is not your enemy

We discussed fear in Chapter Two, "Passion". I wanted this to appear early in the book because, to some extent, fear can be your friend.

Some people fear the mere *thought* of fear. It is well known that people also fear change. So, contrary to popular belief, being close to it means you're probably close to your solution and heading in the right direction. It's not a place you can endure for long, but fear can be a powerful ally if you can control it.

As quoted before, fear is the natural habitat of disruption and innovation. As Franklin D Roosevelt said at a significant time of turmoil for his country: '*There is nothing to fear but fear itself.*'

I hope that my insights have added to your own expectation of what could really be achieved — although you know the journey won't be without its trials. Life would be pretty boring and unfulfilling if it were all 'more of the same'. You are an entrepreneur, if not a pioneer in your field, and your profession, industry or service is waiting for you to deliver so that they can follow.

This book may have provided you with some guides to the structure of making change, because change does follow a process. It may have motivated you to take a step back from your current business to ask: 'Is this really working? Is the current model sustainable enough to meet your personal objectives, both lifestyle and financial?' If not, you may need to visit fear to make change.

Fear and change can work to your advantage if you think past them as you seek your future. Whatever you do, make the jump to start. Until you take the first step, you will go nowhere at all. Gain traction in your cause and be firm, indeed confident in your influence and in its focus — and you will be fine.

Disrupt with a purpose

Creativity, leading to innovation, disruption and then delivery, will be achieved only when you have a motive in mind. It might be money. My experience is that being good at what you do brings wealth, rather than the other way round. Recognition might be your motive. Shallow in a way; it is for me. Each of us will have our own motive unique to the situation. But purpose is vital. .

Without purpose, *you* may struggle to follow the thread, let alone your intended end user. Without their ultimate engagement, you may be innovating for no good reason. Why would you? Just because you can? That may be reason enough but your plans still need to add value, to disrupt current thinking, to change perceptions, to inspire the end user, and ultimately the way we do things... until someone updates your idea! If you think someone *could* update your plans quickly, it's a sign that you are probably not disrupting far enough.

Shake your ideas tree again and see what else falls out. The end result may be the better for it.

Take time to revisit your original vision to see if what you have developed remains true to the original cause. Remembering that 'eureka' moment is a good place to start.

Deliver, deliver, deliver!

It can be easy to lose sight of the finishing post when you are immersed in your plans. Only expend energy on what you can influence; save time, and in all likelihood money, in changing only what you can change. But remember, perceived boundaries are for other folk, not for you when you are innovating.

A former boss of mine used to have 'Attitude, Attitude, Attitude' displayed prominently on her pin board at work, declaring that without it, she and the business could not achieve. I have always agreed with this — until now and these revolutionary times. I still very much believe in the necessity for the right attitude to make things happen. She would always argue that people created their own luck. However, I now think the most important words to any disruptive and innovative project are *'Deliver, Deliver, Deliver!'*

Do not underestimate how revolutionary our times are. Technology, fintech, social media, the internet are opportunities that these specific times afford; opportunities that I believe will not be available again in years to come, possibly until a new alternative to the internet is invented. Like the Industrial Revolution of the beginning of the nineteenth century, the base innovations and tenacity of those who invented them will not be seen again.

The newly industrialising world changed forever back then, and with hindsight we know it was not in all cases for the best. Something similar is happening now.

I'll remind you of the following saying:

"Things move along so rapidly nowadays that people saying: 'It can't be done,' are always being interrupted by somebody doing it." — Puck

Don't be surprised if you find yourself being accused of verging on insanity, out of your depth, or just an oddball. Such people imagine that they know how to beat your concept but seem to be doing very little about it — either that or they are just desperate to keep things unchanged. You know the sort of people I mean: they do a lot of nay-saying but little else. By all means keep an eye on them, just in case, but you need to press ahead anyway and make sure *you* are the one setting the pace.

Whatever you do, plan, conceive, direct... deliver, deliver, and deliver! After developing our work over ten years, I grow tired of people continually asserting that they are going to replicate and improve on our work. To some extent I hope they can, so that we can look to improve our own product by building on someone else's innovation.

However, every piece of rhetoric is usually followed by no action. Talk is still, as they say, cheap!

Deliver your model, whatever you do. What you actually bring to launch may not be exactly how you imagined it; you can spend weeks, months, years perfecting it, only to feel as if the opportunity has been missed somehow. But be an early adopter, get your product working, working well (and importantly, back-tested) and do still bring it to market. If it's not perfect, go back and just tweak the parts that you want to improve on.

Client/customer/user feedback may also suggest changes to your product to improve it still further. Thanks to social media it has never been easier for users to provide valuable real-time feedback.

Looking on the positive side, these same tweaks may present an additional marketing opportunity, in the form of upgrades. Don't let the thought of these stall you from getting the innovation out there and into the market. There can be no feedback if there is nothing to feedback on — and if users are all talking about it, good and bad, you need have little concern that your product/model/process will be a success, as long as you listen.

I hope that I have provided you with some inspiration in the progression and delivery of your concept. Whether from the perspective of 'how not to do it' or 'yes I can', if some or all of this book has propelled you forward and provided you with some navigation for your journey, it will have been worth it. Whether you are talking about innovation, creation, disruption... it can feel like travelling a lonely road. I discovered that it's like taking a piece out of your personal self, which is entirely new to the world, nurturing that and then launching it to the world. As I have suggested before, the experience is personally exhausting — but it's exhilarating at the same time.

Which part of innovative history will you be remembered for?

I think the acid test is: *will you be remembered?* In ten, twenty, thirty years' time, will the history books reflect on the work that you are currently undertaking, tracing its path directly to what are today the *future* systems? Will you be seen as Frank Whittle is to jet engine technology, still in use today, or as Trevor Baylis for the wind-up radio, or of course, Sir Tim Berners-Lee for the internet? Some other bright spark may come along and improve the model again after you retire, but that would still be traceable back to *your* eureka moment. The *future* current users will say: "This was based on the 'Joe Bloggs' system of the mid-Teenies." Wouldn't that be awesome?

From an egotistical perspective, I would like to be known as 'the father of online financial advice'. I don't call this an obsession, just a desire, as a legacy to the vocation I have served for over thirty years. Do I think I will achieve it? Maybe not, our company may be too small, but it's not going to stop me trying — or innovating! Having the Fourth Industrial Revolution at your fingertips is, of course, a great help and motivator.

A few questions remain unanswered by this book. That is because they require a vital contribution from the *real* disruptor and innovator: you. Only *you* can put in the hard work to get these answers in your own field of expertise. Applying yourself and the appropriate resources to finding them is down to you. Remember that disruption is the start of the journey, and who knows when and where it will end?

I wish you every success on your own journey. It has been a pleasure to share some of our real life experiences. If nothing else, they will confirm once and for all that you are not alone.

It has been inspirational, having gained the real life experiences, in all their flavours, to share them with you in these pages. It has been an honour to work with like-minded colleagues, both inside and outside our business, over the recent period of our creative journey, who have willingly shared their passion to make what we influence and offer a little bit better. There is a whole world out there that needs you to change it!

Your wisdom, knowledge, capacity, tenacity and enthusiasm can make it happen soon... what are you waiting for?

Conclusion

Scared of something different

Resources

SOURCES:

- Chapters Financial Limited data / SaidSo.co.uk

- Peter Sheahan, *Flip*, Harper Collins 2007

- Joseph A. Schumpeter, Creative Destruction in Economics, Harvard University

- *Quotation from Puck* magazine 1903 *Things move along so rapidly nowadays that people saying: "It can't be done," are always being interrupted by somebody doing it.*

- Elisabeth Kubler-Ross, *On Death and Dying*, Scribner 1997 (originally published 1969)

- John Lydon, *Anger is an Energy,* Simon and Schuster 2014

- *Wheels of disruption, six clusters of financial services innovation*, World Economic Forum

- Robert Skidelsky, *John Maynard Keynes Volume One: Hopes Betrayed 1883-1920,* Taylor & Francis. Also Alfred Marshall

- *Stop Cutting Costs. Start Enhancing Revenue*, TechWhirl.com article by LavaCon Perspectives

- The Harvard Business Review September 2014, *Profits without Prosperity* by William Lazonick.

- *Robotics Making Workers Redundant in China*, Global Business Review April 2015

- Article and study by scholar Mark Perry (August 2015), entitled *The 'Netflix Effect': An Excellent Example of 'Creative Destruction' AEI.org (American Enterprise Institute)*

- *The Fourth Industrial Revolution*, World Economic Forum 2016

- Raymond Vernon, *International Investment and International Trade in the Product Cycle, The Quarterly Journal of Economics* 1966 (the International Product Lifecycle model)

- Planet First / The Planet Mark, www.planetfirst.co.uk

- Office of National Statistics February 2016 (productivity in Britain's financial services sector has fallen significantly since 2009)

- Nokia, FutureWorks 5G use cases and requirements (2014)

Reproduction consent granted with thanks:

- ***20 Cognitive Biases That Screw Up Your Decisions***, Business Insider 26 August 2015, www.businessinsider.com

- ***The First Consolidated Taxonomy of Disruptive Innovation in Financial Services***, World Economic Forum 2016, diagram reproduced from *The Future of Financial Service: How disruptive innovations are structured, provisioned and consumed,* prepared in collaboration with Deloitte, www3.weforum.org/docs/WEF_The_future__ of_financial_services.pdf

Referencing

Chapter One

- Timothy Jay and Kristin Jay (late 2015) indicates that a fluent use of profanity can be a sign of an articulate nature and a deep intelligence. Language Sciences Journal.

www.sciencedirect.com/science/article/pii/S038800011400151X

- *Global Business Review* article April 2015, *Robotics Making Workers Redundant in China*, giving real examples

www.globalbusinessviews.com/?p=7461

Chapter Two

- AEI.org article August 2015, *The 'Netflix effect': an excellent example of 'creative destruction'*

www.aei.org/publication/the-netflix-effect-is-an-excellent-example-of-creative-destruction

Chapter Three

- The drop in the use of cash for electronic payment systems and new and developing wearable tech

www.bbc.co.uk/news/business-32778196

- I understand that the market for personal SIM cards and smartphone market is reaching saturation point. This is exampled by the Androidauthority.com website on the Chinese market in May 2015.

http://www.androidauthority.com/chinas-smartphone-market-reaching-saturation-607405/

Chapter Four

- Are demographics disrupting convention or creating opportunity?

www.bbc.co.uk/news/business-35056530

- KGW Family Law, Surrey

www.kgwfamilylaw.com/divorce

Chapter Six

- The conciliation service ACAS sets out reasonable grounds for refusing an employee's request for compressed hours

www.acas.org.uk/media/pdf/f/e/Code-of-Practice-on-handling-in-a-reasonable-manner-requests-to-work-flexibly.pdf

Chapter Seven

- TechWhirl.com article (November 2014) by LavaCon Perspectives about the implications of a cost-cutting approach

www.techwhirl.com/lavacon-perspective-stop-cutting-costs-start-enhancing-revenue

Chapter Eight

- The Disruptor article, Citywire, November 2015

http://citywire.co.uk/new-model-adviser/news/the-disruptor-why-clients-will-still-need-the-human-touch/a861236

Scared of something different

About the Authors

Keith Churchouse

BA (Hons), FPFS, Chartered Financial Planner

CFP Chartered FCSI

ISO22222 Certified

Having worked in the financial services industry for over a quarter of a century, and qualified to a high level within UK retail financial services, in 2004 Keith set up Chapters Financial Limited, a Chartered Financial Planning company, with Esther Dadswell, in Guildford, Surrey. The company is authorised and regulated by the Financial Conduct Authority.

Keith also completed a BA (Hons) degree in Financial Services in 2007 with Napier University and became a Fellow of the Personal Finance Society in December 2007. In 2008, using Standards International, he was the fourth person in the UK to achieve ISO 22222 Personal Financial Planner status, the British Standard for Personal Financial Planners. Keith also became a Fellow of the Chartered Institute for Securities and Investment in December 2015.

Taking an avid interest in his local Surrey based business community, Keith was chairman of the Guildford Business

Forum of between 2011 and 2014 and also Trustee to various charities over time, including Headway Surrey. At the time of writing, he maintains various directorships of local companies.

Keith has made regular expert comment in the local and national press and has frequently been interviewed on money matters on local, London and national radio over the last decade.

In 2010, Keith detailed his 25 years' experience in retail financial services in his first book, *Sign Here, Here and Here! . . . Journey of a Financial Adviser.*

He has an active social media presence and can be found on Linkedin.com and Twitter as @onlinefinancial.

In addition, he tries to have a life outside work, and enjoys writing books, art, keeping fit by cycling, scuba diving and classic cars and scooters.

Scared of something different

Esther Dadswell

B Eng (Hons), C Eng, MICE, CMgr, MCMI

Esther has had a successful career in Civil Engineering, graduating in 1991 and achieving Chartered status in 1998. In addition to her engineering qualifications, Esther has also passed the Association of Project Managers Practitioners exam, and in 2014 gained Chartered Manager status from the Chartered Management Institute.

Esther brings a wealth of engineering knowledge and experience to our financial planning world. The synergy between the professions of Engineering and Financial Planning is tangible, especially when looking at the requirements for compliance, procedures and quality production.

Holistic financial planning can involve complicated interaction between various planning issues. Ensuring that clear and timely written financial planning advice is delivered on a consistent basis is paramount.

Esther introduced Chapters Financial Limited to the British Standards benchmark for financial planning (ISO22222 Certificate for Personal Financial Planning), having instigated similar procedures in her extensive career in civil engineering, mainly in transport infrastructure in and around London. This is part of her business ethic, that high quality is achievable, measurable and a standard that must be maintained as a matter of course, rather than merely a business aspiration.

Esther also controls our website **www.chaptersfinancial. com**. Updated regularly, this provides the opportunity for our clients to remain informed and updated on the latest topical issues, with links to our latest press comments and Keith Churchouse's regular blog and radio podcast updates. We attract many clients through our website and we believe that this is a testament to the quality of its easy-to-read format and regular update strategy.

Esther is also director of Elevate Guildford Limited (Experience Guildford), a Business Improvement District (BID) Company.

When Esther can drag herself away from work she enjoys swimming, scuba diving and holidays in the sun. She qualified as an Open Water Diver in 2005 (PADI) and Advanced Open Water Diver in 2006 (PADI) and BSAC Sports Diver in 2007.

Bulk Order Form

Scared of Something Different
ISBN 978-0992828127

If you would like to place a bulk order (minimum 10 books) for this book you can enjoy a direct discount of 25% per book (plus postage and packaging)

Item	Each	Quantity	Amount
Scared of Something Different. . . (Discounted Rate from £9.99)	£7.49		
Postage (per 10 paperbacks books)			**£15.00***
	Total		£

Please make cheque and payments payable to:
Churchouse Consultants LLP

Your details:

Name :	
Address :	
Postcode :	
Contact Number/Email :	

Post your order to:
Hadleigh House, 232 High Street, Guildford, Surrey, GU1 3JF

Our contact details for further information:
Tel: *01483 578800*   Fax: 01483 578864

Email: *info@churchouse.com*

www.churchouseconsultants.com

Churchouse Consultants LLP

Hadleigh House,

232 High Street,

Guildford,

Surrey,

GU1 3JF

Lightning Source UK Ltd.
Milton Keynes UK
UKOW06f2353260716

279325UK00001B/1/P